ETHICS

Mel Thompson

TEACH YOURSELF BOOKS

ACKNOWLEDGEMENTS

The author and publishers would like to thank the *Daily Telegraph*, *The Sunday Times*, *The Independent* and Penguin Books for granting permission to use extracts from their publications in this book.

For Celia

For UK orders: please contact Bookpoint Ltd, 39 Milton Park, Abingdon, Oxon OX14 4TD. Telephone: (44) 01235 400414, Fax: (44) 01235 400454. Lines are open from 9.00 – 6.00, Monday to Saturday, with a 24 hour message answering service. Email address: orders@bookpoint.co.uk

For U.S.A. & Canada orders: please contact NTC/Contemporary Publishing, 4255 West Touhy Avenue, Lincolnwood, Illinois 60646 – 1975 U.S.A. Telephone: (847) 679 5500, Fax: (847) 679 2494.

Long-renowned as the authoritative source for self-guided learning – with more than 30 million copies sold worldwide – the *Teach Yourself* series includes over 200 titles in the fields of languages, crafts, hobbies, sports, and other leisure activities.

British Library Cataloguing in Publication Data
A catalogue record for this title is available from The British Library

Library of Congress Catalog Card Number: 94-6841-2

First published in UK 1994 by Hodder Headline Plc, 338 Euston Road, London NW1 3BH

First published in US 1994 by NTC/Contemporary Publishing, 4255 West Touhy Avenue, Lincolnwood (Chicago), Illinois 60646 – 1975 U.S.A.

The 'Teach Yourself' name and logo are registered trade marks of Hodder & Stoughton Ltd in the UK.

Copyright © 1994 Mel Thompson

Printed in Great Britain for Hodder & Stoughton Educational, a division of Hodder Headline Plc, 338 Euston Road, London NW1 3BH by Cox & Wyman Ltd, Reading, Berkshire.

Impression number	17	16	15	14	13	12	11	10	9
Year		2004	2003	2002	2001	2000	1999		

CONTENTS

1
— INTRODUCTION —
The Art of Living

Ethics is about moral choices. It is about the values that lie behind them, the reasons people give for them, and the language they use to describe them. It is about innocence and guilt, right and wrong, and what it means to live a good or bad life. It is about the dilemmas of life, death, sex, violence and money. In studying it, you are challenged to examine what it is that you want in life and what you believe to be worth doing.

Why then have you picked up this book? Presumably because you are interested in moral dilemmas, in what people consider right or wrong, in the way in which they decide how they ought to act, or what their duty is. In other words, you are interested in life! Each day we are bombarded with news of personal choices and their consequences, from the sexual proclivities of the famous to the violence and tragedy of war, and from the sight of those who are starving in an otherwise prosperous world to the casual vandalism and petty crime of inner city streets. The explanations given for them may vary, from the elaborate exposition of a political or economic ideology to the dismissive shrug of the shoulders. We cannot escape from moral issues, even if our own lives are untouched by painful decisions or tinges of guilt.

In this respect, babies are lucky. They feel hungry, or dirty, or wet, and just scream until someone figures out what is wrong and gives them what they need. They don't have the intellectual ability to question how they got into their particular mess, or the steps they need to take to get out of it. They are not morally responsible. One essential difference between a baby and a mature adult is that the adult recognises when there is a problem to be overcome, or a difficult choice to be made, takes action and then accepts responsibility. Ethics is the rational discussion of that process.

In this book we shall be looking at a variety of ethical arguments, from Thomas Aquinas to Nietzsche, from Machiavelli to Hobbes, from Bentham to Kant, testing them out as we apply them to a whole range of moral issues. But first we need to explore just what it is that makes something moral or immoral.

WHAT MAKES SOMETHING MORAL?

Many choices are a straightforward matter of personal prefer-ence, and the actions that spring from them are neither moral or immoral. They only become the subject of moral debate because of the intentions behind them, the results of them, and the values of society or the individual that they reflect.

> *An example:*
>
> Someone asks you 'Shall I wear red or blue?'. This is not a moral question, and, unless they are going to a political rally, your answer will reflect no more than a preference for one colour rather than another.
>
> BUT - What if the person asking is about to take a walk that will lead across a field in which you know there is a particularly unfriendly bull? (Assuming that the bull is not colour blind and hates red!)
>
> The answer now becomes a matter of moral choice. Shall I, out of hatred or mischief, suggest red? If the person is injured or killed, am I to blame? Is the bull guilty, or am I?
>
> If the bull cannot help but charge when it sees red, can it be blamed for doing what comes naturally? If I have a compulsion to cause mischief, which makes it emotionally impossible for me to suggest the safer colour, can I use the same argument to claim my own innocence? If not, then

what degree of freedom (psychological, emotional, physical) renders me morally responsible? And are we free, anyway, if every factor is fully taken into account? A close friend, seeing the glint in my eye as my lips frame the word 'red', might comment 'I just knew you'd say that!'.

What if I know the bull is in the field, but refuse to suggest which colour the person should wear? Do I bear any moral responsibility for the consequences of withholding that information? Does it make any difference if I hope that they will be hurt, or am indifferent? Am I less guilty by taking a passive rather than an active part in the decision?

This example shows that a central question for ethics is that of freedom. If we are not free to choose what we do, we cannot be held morally responsible for our actions.

But the situation also illustrates another feature of moral responsibility. Our freedom to choose is often limited by the choices that others make, and our moral responsibility is therefore proportional to the degree to which our choice is significant. In this situation, I take greater responsibility, because the bull was not free to choose whether or not to charge. Where freedom is shared more equally, a person's contribution can be seen positively ('aiding and abetting') or negatively ('contributory negligence'). We shall be looking in more detail at the issue of freedom in Chapter 2.

Actions can be divided into three categories:

1. Moral - if they reflect a person's values and those of society.

2. Immoral - if they go against a person's (or society's) values.

3. Amoral - if they are not based on values or social norms.

(Of course, an individual may think that something is moral, even if the rest of society thinks it immoral. Doing something immoral is not the same thing as breaking the law. Actions can be moral but illegal, or immoral but legal.)

Whether you think an action is moral or immoral will depend on your values and the ethical arguments you use to decide what is right. How many actions or choices are moral and how many relegated to the general 'amoral' category will depend on your moral sensitivity, the range of values to which you consciously subscribe, and whether you belong to a society which operates by definite rules and values. (When faced with a restaurant menu, a newly convinced vegetarian with a residual passion for meat will have more moral dilemmas than a cheerful omnivore. A hungry Jew or Muslim will have added problems if faced with pork, and for some Buddhists and Hindus, eating meat may threaten to undermine their whole view of the value of living creatures. A crucial moral question for one person may be of negligible significance to another.)

Most moral situations are not straightforward. They may involve personal values and needs, common sense, the Law, and a whole range of unknown consequences. Unlike the student of ethics, who may review the intentions behind and results of an action at his or her leisure, moral dilemmas often involve instant decisions.

The moral issues contained in a situation may depend not so much on what actually happens, as on the intention and the appropriateness of what is done.

An example:

A masked stranger makes you lie on a table, drugs you into unconsciousness, takes out a sharp knife and slices into your naked body. Is the action moral, immoral or amoral?

At this point you might well want to know if the person with the knife is a competent surgeon or a student of the Marquis de Sade! A description of the action itself is not necessarily the best guide to its moral consequences. You might therefore ask:

• Is this a qualified surgeon?

• Have I consented to this operation?

• Is it likely to benefit me?

• Have the implications of it been explained to me?

- If he is not a surgeon, do I want him to continue?

  (It might, after all, be an emergency, and an unqualified surgeon might be better than none.)

- What are his motives for doing this operation? (Money? Genuine altruism?)

- If his motives were other than these (e.g. sexual gratification) would I still want him to continue, if I believed that it would also be for my benefit?

The situation described above has to do with relationships, agreements between parties, intentions, and possible outcomes. It is these things, rather than the straight description of the action that is performed, that decides whether it is right or wrong.

Facts alone do not decide the morality of a situation and a moral statement must include more than facts.

'People are dying of starvation in Somalia' is not a moral statement. But if you add '... and you are doing nothing to help', then it becomes a moral issue, if the person addressed is actually in a position to help and is not doing so.

In other words, a moral statement is about choice and intention, about self-understanding and about the vision and view one has of the world.

— WHAT IS THE POINT OF ETHICS? —

Ethics is the systematic study of moral choices, but does this actually help with moral choice? Would it not be better to be guided by conscience tempered with a little pragmatism and set aside all theorising?

Well, I suppose most people know what it is to make a moral choice, and then be left wondering if their decision was right, if they acted with real conviction or merely from an emotional whim, if they acted with integrity, or if they will come to regret it. What seems right in some circumstances may, in the cold light of another day, seem particularly foolish.

Yet there are two images of the person who is concerned about ethics, one positive and one negative, but both potentially creative:

• A person launches out on a moral quest (and for most people it will remain a quest, rather than an achievement) for maturity and integrity. To act with conviction; to act decisively; to see clearly where you are going; to set goals; to cut through the confusions of life by doing what you are convinced is right and by being able to justify your actions. This quest is for a life freed from debilitating uncertainty; it is for a life that is more creative and decisive.

• A person is sitting alone, head in hands, asking 'How did I get into this mess?'.

The second of these is a good starting point. The first sets an ideal goal, except that some people who pretend to have achieved it remain coldly certain of themselves, a little brittle perhaps. Not easy people to live with, those who are always right! The study of ethics offers the balance between these two images; it helps people to find direction, and to act with conviction, but (by showing the whole variety of decisions that can be made, and the reasons for them) it promotes empathy with those who struggle with moral dilemmas, and suggests that humility is the most realistic basis for the voicing of moral opinions.

In practical terms, the study of ethics can offer two things. First of all, it helps people to appreciate the choices that others make, and to evaluate their justification of them. But secondly, it involves a reflective sharpening of people's own moral awareness, a conscious examination of their values and choices, of how these have shaped their life so far, and (more importantly) of how they can use them to shape their lives in the future.

You already know far more about ethics than you might realise. For although 'Ethics', as a subject to be studied, uses philosophical terms, its basis is in the common sense which, consciously or unconsciously, people use all the time in deciding what to do. This book will therefore look at commonsense choices in a systematic way.

You don't have to know the term 'utilitarian' in order to want to do what seems to have a chance of giving the greatest happiness to the greatest number of people. Therefore, although this book will outline theories of ethics, and the terms that are used in ethical debate, it will be important to examine these in the context of actual choices that people make.

Some choices are obvious; others are more problematic. It is by looking at the problematic ones that we start to appreciate the issues involved in all ethical debate.

A *situation:*

(From a report of the trial at the Old Bailey, London, in March 1990)

A businessman, aged 37, learns that he is dying of cancer. His business is failing, and he is concerned to provide for his wife after his death. He therefore plants six small home-made bombs in supermarkets in Germany. He contacts the supermarket company, claims that 35 devices have been planted and demands £300,000 to reveal their whereabouts. He is arrested after making telephone negotiations from a call box in London, and admits blackmailing and possession of explosive substances. The bombs cause £100,000 of damage, but no injuries. In court, his defence counsel claims that he acted out of a genuine sense of desperation, and asks that the sentence might be short enough for him to end his life with his family. He is sentenced to a prison term of two and a half years.

* Was the businessman justified in attempting the blackmail in order to provide for his wife?

* If the blackmail had succeeded, he might have argued that insurance would have covered the losses, and that no individual would have been hurt by his action. It is right to cheat an institution for the benefit of an individual?

* The judge is reported to have said 'What I have to do is to impose a sentence which will reflect that part of the balance of your life it is proper for you to spend in custody'. Do you agree with this approach, and with the

---

sentence given? If not, what would you think appropriate?

• If the wife knew of the plans, would she be in the wrong for not stopping him?

• If she did not know, but his plan had succeeded, would she have been right to keep the money if she subsequently found out how it had been obtained?

This situation illustrates four different features of ethical debate:

1. It shows that moral decisions are based on values. The businessman considered his wife's future security more valuable than the financial loss to a chain of supermarkets.

2. It can be examined in terms of what is known as a 'utilitarian' argument: the expected results of the action are weighed. The considerable gain by one person (the wife) is balanced by an equal loss, but shared between many people.

3. It introduces the problems of how you decide what is an appropriate punishment for a crime, and what the purpose of punishment is to be.

4. It illustrates a central moral dilemma – do you live by general rules (e.g. it is wrong to attempt to get money by deception), or do you allow an individual situation to be the sole basis of what is the appropriate thing to do, (i.e. that his dying and his wife's need is a situation which demands special action, and this takes precedence over any general moral rules).

Ethics tends to go round in a circle. You start by observing the moral choices people make and the reasons they give for them. From these you can devise theories – say what you think Ethics is really about. But then you return to actual moral choices, and look at them more carefully in the light of the theories you have considered.

Maturity is about taking responsibility for your own life; about taking decisions; about asking 'Why?', rather than just screaming, when things go wrong. Maturity is seen in the values that a person has, and the way in which they are applied to his or her situation. In many ways, maturity is what the whole of ethics is about: the question of what it is to think and act in a way that reflects the full stature of a rational human being. A central feature of this is integrity.

——— WHAT PRICE INTEGRITY?———

Much of ethics is about integrity. It is about applying basic values to the decision making process, and therefore living in a way that allows your personality to be expressed in what you do. But at what price? One of the hazards of taking Ethics seriously, and of trying to live up to your personal values, is that you may have to take the consequences. Think about those people who are determined to live with integrity. Do they necessarily have the most comfortable or hassle-free life? Those who risk their own lives in order to save others? Those who publicly expose corruption? Those who campaign for human rights in a country where they are systematically denied? Their consciences may be clear, but could you live with a slightly uneasy conscience for the sake of ...

Often it is a matter of scale. If a moderately well-off person is offered a quick, risk free way of making £10 through some morally dubious scheme, he or she might well refuse. But what if the same scheme involved millions of pounds? If it promised to benefit not just yourself but many other people as well? When the stakes are very high, integrity (and the morality that it entails) become expensive!

An example:

Let us look at an example connected with the two great motivaters, sex and money. If you were to be offered £20 to have sex with someone you do not particularly like, you could well afford to take a moral line (e.g. that, as a matter of principle, you will only have sex with someone you like, and that you will certainly not set aside that principle, and therefore your integrity, for the sum of £20). You therefore decline the offer. But what if you were desperate and hungry? What if you were on the streets (literally) with no means of support? Compared with the need for food, shelter and £20, sex might be regarded as an inconvenient necessity of survival. You could argue that your integrity requires that your own survival, and perhaps that of other desperate people who are totally dependent on you, should take precedence over your sexual preferences. There are many places where prostitution is undertaken for just such reasons. How does that change the moral nature of the act?

Or change the scale of rewards on offer:

There is someone who has fallen in love with you, but you do not find him or her attractive. On the other hand, he or she is wealthy: this relationship will provide you will all that you have ever dreamed of. Might it not be worth a little pretence? Might you not feel that you really could 'fake it', for years if necessary, for the sake of all that? Might it not be possible, you argue, justifying your decision, that you will eventually get to like this wealthy partner?

If the pretence involved in this last example strikes you as immoral, it shows where integrity comes on your personal scale of values. The crucial test, however, is the choice between integrity and survival; to choose death rather than loss of integrity is the basic question behind every martyrdom, from Socrates, through centuries of religious persecution, to those who agree to give testimony against criminals or terrorists, knowing that they risk their lives doing so.

— RIGHTS AND RESPONSIBILITIES —

So far we have been looking at individual moral choices, but there is another side to ethics. Much discussion in ethics is about the rights that a person should have. In other words, what they can reasonably expect society to do for them, and what they are expected to contribute to society in exchange. These are embodied in, for example, the United Nations Universal Declaration of Human Rights. We assume that, in a civilised society, people will be treated in a way which respects their basic needs (as in the

American Constitution) for life, liberty and the pursuit of happiness. Where there are gross violations of these basic rights, we may recoil in horror. We say 'It shouldn't be allowed!' but are then forced to recognise that there may be nobody able to enforce those standards – that torture, execution or genocide can happen in that place. Innocent people are allowed to be killed. Society does not act to impose a moral standard, either because it cannot, or because it will not.

Looking at society as a whole we can ask:

• What rights should a person have?

• What responsibilities should you accept?

• Do you have a duty to fulfil a certain role in society?

In other words, what can we expect of other people, and what can they expect of us? What is it that makes a society 'civilised'?

Such questions take us beyond the world of personal choice. They ask about the way in which society works, and how what we do affects others. In Chapter 8, we shall be looking at some specific examples of the way in which society copes with those whose values and choices cause harm to others, and the way in which it imposes punishments upon individuals.

But not all rules imposed by society are necessarily moral. In Britain a person is required to drive on the left-hand side of the road. In the United States, the same person is required to drive on the right. That is a social convention. Obeying it is not a matter of morality. Social etiquette and convenience are not the same thing as social morality, even though they can influence behaviour. They only become the subject of moral debate when they concern matters of value, and imply general views about the purpose and nature of human life.

For reflection:

In the autumn of 1992, a Symphony of Sorrowful Songs was recorded. It was by the little known Polish composer, Henryk Gorecki, a man who had walked into Auschwitz concentration camp as a child, and realised that the shingle

---

of the paths under his feet were the bones of the dead. A film was shown on television in Britain in the spring of 1993 in which, during a performance of the symphony, images of the orchestra and soloist were intercut with shots of the gas chambers, the heaps of corpses being dragged out for burial, the ovens. Then, as the symphony progressed, more recent images were added: the bodies of children gassed in Iraq, the skeletal living in starving Sudan. Then there was film of two men sitting on the ground, surrounded by their captors, you see one of them kicked in the head, putting his hand up in a helpless gesture of self-protection; you watch as the other man is systematically battered with a hammer, you wonder how can he continue to live through all this. Yet, shakily, he manages to sit up again, only to be struck again. You are watching the banal brutality of the captors. You see the dehumanised helplessness of the victims. You ask 'Why?'. How can people do this to one another? Are there no rights? Is there no international law that can prevent such barbarism? Once a regime gains power, whether local or national, can it simply set aside all the norms of civilised behaviour?

And over these scenes, the songs are of a woman mourning for her lost son. The music and the images reinforce one another, asking the terrible questions 'Is this really what human life is like? Could I, in different circumstances, find myself imposing this cruelty? Is this the truth about what we are all capable of doing?

In asking these questions, we have already started the process of ethical debate; we have asked about laws and rights; we sense instinctively that certain actions are wrong, no matter what the circumstances; we feel numbed by the sheer scale of human suffering.

Having rights is about being respected as a human individual, and that is the starting point of almost all ethical theories.

THE ART OF LIVING

A work of art is something created, by inspiration, by intuition, by a sense of balance, by a thoughtful use of the media available. It offers more than a simple view of canvas, paint, stone or whatever else has been used. It may be minimalist, saying something through its very simplicity. It may be rich in symbolism or colour or form, complex and challenging. But whatever it is, a work of art is the deliberate product of a mind. It is an attempt to 'say something', to express meaning, or value, or hope. It is an attempt to probe beneath the banal and the superficial.

'Ethics' can be limited to a study of the meaning of moral language, but more broadly it is what used to be called 'moral philosophy': the study of moral choices and the arguments that spring from them. It is with this broader sense of 'ethics' that this book is mainly concerned. We can therefore say that ethics is about the art of living – seeing your life as the material out of which, through the choices you make, you are gradually constructing a work of art. You are more than flesh, bones and mortgages. You cannot be defined by your financial, work, social or political status. You are not simply a consumer. You are not an unthinking slave of a society. You are not an automaton, programmed by genetic, environmental and social factors. You have feelings, intuitions, dreams, ambitions. These you reveal in the choices you make. Through your choices, you shape your life; you practise the art of living.

For reflection:

It is worth pausing to reflect upon the conscious choices that we have made, and the ways in which they have shaped our lives. Career; marriage; family relationships; political allegiances; financial choices – all express values and commitments that we held at the time we made those choices. Some we may now regret, others remain central to our understanding of life.

These personal choices, as much as the dramatic life-and-death decisions, are important for an understanding of Ethics. They shape our character, they influence our values, and they set precedents for choices that we will make in the future. They may contribute to the forming of our habitual attitude to life, an attitude which may determine what we do when faced with a moment of crisis and serious moral choice.

Our lives are continually being shaped by the choices we make, and by the convictions and values that underlie them. In this way, our lives are like works of art. We can take the material of life and either react to it in a passive way, always remaining life's victim, or we can take it and use it creatively.

But what has this to do with a more usual list of moral issues?

• Should I have an abortion?

• Should I help these people to die if they are in pain?

• Should I join the army or be a pacifist?

• Should I take advantage of someone else's miscalculation?

You may choose to think through all these things (and this book will encourage you to do just that), but if you are faced with one of these choices, especially if the stakes are very high, your choice may not be based on rational thought alone. It will be based, in all probability, on the cumulative effect of many other choices that you have made over the years. Fundamentally, it will be based on what the 'work of art' that is your life is actually trying to 'say'. It will be based on your image of yourself and your (perhaps unconscious) convictions about life.

The task of Ethics is to assist people in looking at these images, evaluating them and shaping them through reflecting on a range of moral issues. It aims to help people to make their moral choices with conviction and clarity of mind, and to adopt a positive and creative attitude towards them.

A situation:

One day ....

You cannot escape Ethics if you read the newspapers. So, as an introduction to this study of creative decision making, take a look at a daily newspaper. Go through it listing the news items and features which involve some sort of moral decision, against each of them jot down your own views and (if you wish at this stage) the sort of argument that you would use to justify those views. Of course, it would be interesting to get two very different newspapers and see how the moral issues they present vary. One might lead on the sex life of someone well known, another might comment on an economic or political crisis, but both raise moral issues.

As an example, here is the front page of the *Daily Telegraph* for Thursday March 4th 1993. It's not a newspaper I buy regularly. I just happened to be given it on the day when I sat down to plan the introduction to this book. It has not been chosen for its rich moral content – like most things in life, it is just the one that happens to be at hand at a significant moment, and we are left to make of it what we can.

Thousands flee onslaught by Serbs

The United Nations security council has an emergency meeting as reports come in of indiscriminate killings and thousands of refugees, as Bosnian Serbs attack Muslim areas – just part of a mess that was the former Yugoslavia.

- Should the UN get involved in the internal affairs of a country, even one in which order has broken down?

- How do you solve present problems, when old hatreds, rivalries and misunderstandings go back generations?

- Do you send in relief supplies to both sides in a war, or only the side you want to support?

- Apparently, those who tried to get at relief supplies that had dropped outside their own areas came under enemy fire as they did so? Is it ever right, in war, to prevent humanitarian aid from getting through?

Princess says 'I shall never complain again'.

The Princess of Wales visited a small village hut in Nepal, and responded in this way to the poverty of the people there.

- Should everyone have the same share of money and goods?

- If a culture is based on the simplicity and poverty of rural life, is it right to try to 'develop' it? What happens when you attempt to impose Western city cultures upon the under-developed nations?

- How should you give aid?

Three more held in IRA hunt

- When, if ever, is violence justified?

- If you have no other way of changing a political system, is it right to carry out terrorist activities against a civilian population?

- Should the death penalty be retained for those who carry out terrorist crimes?

- Given the unsafe nature of some earlier convictions (e.g. those of the so-called 'Guildford Four' and 'Birmingham Six') how do you make certain that suspects are given a fair trial?

Optimism over economy rises

Economic matters are not usually associated directly with ethics, but, in fact, how you run an economy depends directly on the values you hold and the attitude you have to wealth and development.

- One person's cut in mortgage payments is another person's drop in investment income. Fine, perhaps, if those with mortgages are thought of as young and poor, and those with investments as wealthy. Not quite so clear where the mortgage is huge, and has been taken on as a means to speculate on the rise in property prices, and the person with the investment is a pensioner with a very small additional income.

- Sometimes it sounds as if a rise in the economy is a reward for moral effort, and that someone is at fault if it declines.

- Perhaps this item raises an issue similar to that encountered by the Princess in the Nepalese hut – can we expect a certain standard of living as of right?

Other small news items on the front page include:

Sect leader 'told by God to wait'

After four Federal agents from the US Customs agency are shot dead by members of the Branch Davidian sect in Waco, Texas, there is a siege. The leader of the sect refuses to surrender, but waits for further instructions from God. All sorts of moral dilemmas here:

- The sect has many guns and heavy weapons. But these can be bought easily in the USA. Should there be more control on the sale of firearms? Should everyone have the right to carry a weapon? (Texas has no gun registration laws, and in 1992 it was the only state in the US in which more people were shot dead than killed in road accidents.) How do you decide what is adequate for self-defence? If you are leader of a sect that thinks the end of the world is coming soon, and that there will be a final bloody war between the forces of good and evil, is a heavy machine-gun quite reasonable as a means of self defence?

Charities oppose 'sin bins' plan

The Home Secretary proposes detention centres for persistent young offenders. Some charities claim that this will not solve the problem of youth crime.

- At the moment, a person in the UK has to take moral responsibility for his or her actions from the age of 10. Is that reasonable? How should young people be punished? Should the families of young offenders become involved in their punishment and rehabilitation?

- When a 10-year-old is charged with murder, who is really to blame?

- What about the influence of violent films on TV and video?

- Frustration; social deprivation: are these mitigating circumstances?

Athlete 'positive'

This refers to Ben Johnson, the Canadian sprinter, who had already been excluded from the 1988 Olympics because of a drugs offence, now accused of taking another illegal substance which might be thought to aid his sporting performance.

- Every technique is intended to help an athlete gain the edge over his or her opponents. Why should some of these be made illegal? Should special diets be allowed, or should all athletes have to eat the same food in order to make their competition fair? What about drugs and treatments that have not yet been branded as illegal? When the law catches up with them, will penalties be imposed retrospectively?

Serious comment on the issues raised on that single front page involve many of the central concerns of ethics. Without ethical thought, you would be unable to comment at all. The fact that you are likely to have views on some, if not all, of these things indicates just how broad is your own set of moral views – and the reasons you give for your comments reflect your own ethics.

2

– FREE TO CHOOSE? –

—— WHAT KIND OF FREEDOM? ——

Nobody is completely free to do anything that he or she may wish. Freedom is limited in different ways:

- I may decide that I would like to launch myself into the air, spread my arms and fly. I may have dreamed of doing so. I may have a passion for Superman films, and feel certain that in some way it should be possible. But my physical body is, and will always be, incapable of unaided flight. To overcome that limitation, I must resort to technology.

- I may wish to be a famous and highly talented artist, musician or gymnast, but my freedom is again limited. It may not be physically impossible for me to achieve these things, but it requires such a level of experience, training and natural ability, that my chances of achieving what I want are severely restricted.

- I may wish to go to London and parade myself naked before Buckingham Palace. There is no physical limitation to inhibit me and no great skill required, but I am likely to be arrested.

These are examples of limitation to actual freedom. Whether by physical laws, natural abilities, or legal or social restraints, we are all limited in what we can do.

If I am to make a moral choice, I must be free to do, or not to do, the thing in question. It cannot be morally wrong of me not to fly, because I am unable to do so. On the other hand, walking about naked in public could become a moral issue, if it was argued that I had done so in order to give offence, simply because I was free to choose whether or not I did so.

FREE WILL

It is important to make the distinction between freedom in general and freedom of the will.

I may look at various options, and think that I am free to choose between them. Someone who knows me well may, on hearing my decision, say 'I just knew you'd choose to do that!'. Is it possible for my will to be free, for it to be possible for me to weigh up all the factors involved and come to a genuinely free choice, and yet for someone else to be able to predict accurately what I will do? (And it won't be any use changing my mind at the last minute, or acting out of character, because those things too could be predicted.)

There is something intensely irritating about people saying that they know exactly what you will freely choose to do. This is because, in the moment of choice, we experience freedom. And that freedom is important to us. Robots and computers may be totally predictable, but most humans are convinced that they themselves are not.

Consider the following cases of murder:

1. A thief shoots and kills a bank clerk in the course of a raid.

2. A husband or wife kills his or her partner after years of provocation and unhappiness.

3. A young man rapes and kills a girl whom he has not met before, on account of his particularly violent sexual urges.

4. A psychopath, unwisely released from a secure hospital to live in the community, kills someone for no apparent reason, does not attempt to conceal the crime, and shows no remorse when apprehended and charged with murder.

All four have killed another human being. But are they all equally guilty in a moral sense? Do any of them have genuine grounds for having the charge of murder reduced to that of manslaughter, for example?

- It is assumed that the bank robber freely chooses to carry a weapon. Even if the actual shot were the result of being startled by a sudden movement, for example, that does not detract significantly from the general view that his act was murder, because he exercised freedom of the will in deciding to carry a loaded weapon.

- With domestic murder, there may be a significant element of provocation. In that case, especially if the murder takes place in the course of a heated argument, it might be argued that the victim contributed to the situation that brought about the crime, or that (if sufficiently provoked) the murder took place while the person concerned was temporarily deranged. He or she might be charged with manslaughter on the grounds of diminished responsibility.

- The issue in the case of the sexual murder is one of the freedom of the murderer to decide whether or not to act on his sexual impulses. If it can be shown that the condition is such that the young man is not in control of himself in certain situations, then psychiatric reports would be relevant evidence to bring before the court.

- In the case of the psychopath, it is recognised that he or she is not in control of his or her actions, and does not respond to the normal inhibitions and rational constraints that apply to those who are sane.

Two situations:

A woman suffering from schizophrenia stabbed and killed a worker in the hostel into which she had moved on discharge from hospital. In May 1993, she was found not-guilty of murder on grounds of insanity. She claimed to believe that her victim was the antichrist.

In another case, a plea of manslaughter was accepted because 'his responsibility at the time of the killing was

---

substantially impaired as a result of schizophrenic illness and / or psychopathic personality disorder' but that 'that mental state was likely to have been compounded by abuse of crack cocaine and alcohol.'

In the first of these, the plea for insanity seems straightforward. But in the second, there is the secondary use of drugs.

- Does this mean that the person is morally responsible, because the acceptance of drugs (as opposed to his illness) was a freely chosen act?

- Is it reasonable to argue that someone with that degree of mental disturbance is not responsible for choosing whether or not to take drugs?

In each case, the law accepted a charge of manslaughter. But is there any moral responsibility here? Does it lie with the killer, or with the social situation that allows the killer to be in a situation where their lack of normal restraint can lead to such harm?

- In what sense were either of them free?

Notice that the issue here is one of freedom of the will. The psychopath is certainly not free to choose how to act. But is the man with the uncontrollable sexual urge free? Or the provoked wife? In each case we have to examine personal, psychological and social factors.

There may be a great deal of vandalism in areas of high unemployment. Does that imply that the unemployed are less able to exercise complete freedom in terms of what they do? Are social pressures enough to justify actions which can be regarded by other people as morally wrong?

There are extreme situations, of course, where the pressure on a person is so great, that he or she feels that there is no freedom to act otherwise. Unlike the psychopath, he or she is fully aware of the implications of the choices involved, but the need to act in a particularly way is overwhelming. This is a loss of freedom, but not of freedom of the will. An extreme example of this is where it concerns life and death.

An example:

Survivors of a plane crash in the Andes realise that they will die unless they get food. The only possibility is to eat the flesh of those of their number who have already died. Some refuse, and die. Others, reluctantly, eat the flesh, and many of them survive.

The fact that some of them are able to make the choice not to eat shows that the survivors can still exercise freedom of the will.

- But if the only option is death, then, in practical terms, freedom is severely limited.

- In these circumstances, can cannibalism be regarded as a morally acceptable choice?

One particularly interesting example of the way in which freedom can be limited is that of blackmail or hostage taking. In the case of blackmail, there may well be three different moral situations involved:

1. The blackmailer is trying to limit the freedom of his or her victim, which is a moral (most would say 'immoral') act.

2. The person being blackmailed may be required to do something which he or she regards as morally wrong.

3. But the person being blackmailed may also act out of fear that some other action from his or her past will be exposed if he or she does not comply with the blackmailer's demands; the acceptance of responsibility for this act creates the third moral dilemma.

Hence, the blackmail victim has three choices:

1. To admit to whatever past action the blackmailer is threatening to expose.

2. Go public on the blackmail, which may also involve an admission of the action for which he or she is being blackmailed.

3. Do what the blackmailer says.

Where there is hostage taking, or blackmail that will affect the lives of others, then the pressure to conform with the blackmailer's demands may be even greater.

A *situation:*

The manager of a supermarket is attacked in his home. His attackers want him to take money from his own supermarket and deliver it to them. His wife and two children are held hostage. He is told that they will be harmed if he fails to carry out the orders he has been given.

- As he drives to the supermarket that morning, is he free to choose what he will do?

- Should he be morally blamed for taking the money and handing it over?

- If he informs the police and his wife or children are harmed as a result, who is to blame for that harm? Does he share the blame with the thieves who actually carried it out, on the grounds that he could have prevented it by following their instructions?

Blackmail, whether it is of an emotional or physical variety, is the attempt to take from a person the freedom of his or her will. In fact, however, this does not actually happen. A person who is being blackmailed is still free to choose whether or not to conform to the blackmailer's demands. The difference is that the values expressed in, and the likely consequences of, whatever it is that the blackmailer is demanding, provides a person with a new set of criteria for deciding what to do.

In the case given above, if there had been no threat, the supermarket manager would have been in a position to balance the benefit of having a large sum of money against the likelihood of being caught stealing from his shop, and his sense of honesty and loyalty to his company. In such circumstances, he would probably choose not to steal – which is what happened on every other day as he went to work. On the other hand, if the choice is between the death or injury of wife and children on the one hand, and stealing from the company on the other, then – even if he were to be caught, blamed and given a long prison sentence – he might judge it the better of the two options open to him.

What is being taken away from him is the freedom to act without duress, **not** the freedom of the will as such. The choice for the supermarket manager is therefore still a moral one.

─── DETERMINISM ───

Science is based on the observation of cause and effect, and the formulation of general principles by which events may be predicted.

You look up and say 'I think it's going to rain'. You do not thereby imply that the weather has a personality, and that you guess that it has decided to enjoy a little precipitation. Rather, you make an observation based on the clouds, wind, dampness in the air, and also on your observation of similar things leading to rain on previous occasions.

- The falling of rain is determined absolutely by certain atmospheric conditions.

- The fact that you may be inaccurate in predicting those conditions, and therefore the coming of the rain, does not detract from the fundamentally determined nature of that event.

- Given certain conditions, there will be rain. Without them there cannot be rain. The weather is determined. Its absolute prediction is theoretically possible, even if practically difficult.

The prediction of rain is possible because it is recognised that all physical phenomena are causally connected. Everything from the weather to the electrical impulses within human brains can be explained in terms of physical laws.

From the rise of modern science in the 17th century to the early part of the 20th century, it could be said with some certainty that science was mechanistic. The whole world was seen as a machine, knowledge of which would enable mankind to predict and control the action of individual things. Even the process of evolution, as set out by Darwin, had a mechanistic and determinist basis. With the theory of natural selection, we have a clear example of the way in which change is forced forward through the operation of an impersonal law; that only those who survive to adulthood are able to breed, and it is they, rather than others of the species, who will determine the future.

Although, of course, in the general run of things, science still appears to be largely deterministic, some philosophers have made much of the fact that in quantum mechanics, for example, things sometimes happen in a random way. Overall trends can be seen, but the action of individual quanta cannot be predicted. At the sub-atomic level, it is also noted that the very act of observing some phenomena causes them to change, so it is not possible to formulate and test out physical laws with quite the crude certainty that prevailed in the last century.

Nevertheless, overall, including the spheres of sociology and psychology, which come closest to the issues with which morality has to deal, science has retained a largely determinist viewpoint. There is a general acceptance that all events (including human action) may be explained in terms of prior events which are seen to cause them. And in the case of human action, this may be explained to a significant extent at least, in terms of the effect of environment or upbringing on the individual.

An Example:

There is a car accident, the car swerves across the road and collides with a tree, killing the driver.

You can trace back the origins of everything involved, from the growth and planting of the tree, to the manufacture of the car. But what were the significant factors? Why did the car swerve? Did a tyre burst? If so, how worn was it? Was there a fault in its manufacture? Was there a steering fault? If so, was it a design fault? (Accidents in which damage is made worse through a design fault can lead to the manufacturer being prosecuted, for having contributed to the accident.)

What if you trace everything – from the skill of the driver, to the food that he or she has been eating (was the driver faint? sick? drunk?) to whether the tree should have been planted so close to the road? The driver may have had control over some of these things, but not over others. Yet everything that has ever happened can contribute is some way to each single event. Is anyone to blame? What if the road had not been built? What if cars had not been invented .... ?

If we had total knowledge of every event up to the moment of the crash, then everything would be seen to fit a seamless patters of cause and effect.

But the experience of that event (for the driver before dying and for those who know him, or witness it) will be different. There may be guilt feelings. People may wish that other decisions had been made. There is an inescapable sense that the events are somehow influenced by human choice. Without that, there would be no sense of morality.

We may be socially or psychologically predisposed to act in a certain way, as a the result of upbringing or environment. Even more direct is the influence of our genetic make-up, for scientists examining 'behaviourial genetics' have suggested that genes could well give a predisposition to violence, depression, schizophrenia or homosexuality.

If it could be shown that there was a direct causal link, then the case for determinism in these areas of life would be strengthened. On the other hand, whereas physical traits, e.g. the colour of one's eyes, are 100 per cent due to heredity, studies of twins have suggested that behavioural factors, such as homosexuality, can have a heredity factor as low as 31 per cent. This illustrates what common sense would suggest, that there are other factors as well as our genes that influence our behaviour. This does not, however, disprove a claim that everything is determined. It merely shows that there are a number of factors working together to produce a particular result. No one of them can be shown to determine the final result, but taken together they do so, each contributing something to the determinist equation.

An example:

Two recent studies suggest a biological predisposition to homosexuality. Professor Simon DeVay of the Salk Institute in San Diego, California, published a study in 1991 suggesting that the part of the brain responsible for sexual behaviour is smaller in women and homosexuals than in heterosexual men. Then, in 1993, a team led by Dr Hamer of the National Institutes of Health in Bethesda, Maryland, published its study into the genetic predisposition to homosexuality.

If either or both of these studies are correct, what are their moral implications?

- If homosexuality is physically or genetically determined, does that imply that sexual preferences are not a matter for moral debate?

- For those who are anxious about their sexual orientation, it may alleviate a sense of guilt, instilled by social or religious opposition to homosexuality – for it is difficult to see how a person can be held responsible for his or her genetic constitution.

- If a simple blood test could show homosexual orientation, and if that test could be carried out on a foetus early in pregnancy, would that be a sufficient reason for abortion, if the parents felt that they did not want homosexual offspring? And if so, on what moral grounds could it be argued?

- If varieties of behaviour (whether sexual or otherwise) are due to genes, should all forms of behaviour be accepted as of equal value? If not, on what basis do you hold that some are right and others wrong?

It would seem that, even if there could be shown to be absolute genetic determinism, that would not in itself remove all moral issues.

These things influence not just our freedom, but the freedom of our will. We may think we are free to choose what we do, but the psychologist, sociologist or behavioural geneticist observing us claims to know better.

——————— REDUCTIONISM ———————

Reductionism is a philosophical rather than an ethical problem, but it does highlight an extreme form of determinism, and one which makes moral language, and the whole idea of personal freedom, meaningless.

I move a muscle; my arm is raised. My experience of the reasoning behind that action is that I want to pick up my pen to write. But an analysis of what is actually happening is quite different.

- The muscle contracts because there is a chemical change.

- The chemical change is brought about through stimuli passing through nerve cells.

- The tiny electrical impulses in the nerves originate in the brain.

- The brain contains many millions of electrical circuits. For every movement of the body and thought passing through the mind, there is the corresponding electrical impulse in the brain.

If you pass an electric charge across my brain, I will twitch my muscles involuntarily. If the blood supply to part of the brain is cut off, those brain cells will die, and as a result parts of my body will cease to operate normally (as happens when someone has a cerebral thrombosis). In this case, I will not be aware that the damage is in my brain. All I will know is that my leg will not work.

Now this leads a reductionist to claim that the thoughts we have are 'nothing but' electrical impulses. Freedom of the will is therefore an illusion in two ways – firstly, it is theoretically possible to predict any choice, and secondly, that choice is actually nothing more than a set of electrical impulses which follow the laws of physics.

Against this one could argue that such reductionism is like saying that a book is nothing other than a collections of letters printed on paper, or that a paining is nothing but a collection of bits of pigment on canvas. Whatever physical analysis a reductionist may offer, my experience of the book or of the painting is of something **more than** their material bases. For moral choice (and therefore ethics) to make any sense, I have to believe that a person is more than determined electrical impulses.

I cannot perceive the working of my brain, because my perception (and I myself, as a self-conscious agent) are the product of that brain operation. There is nothing I can do that does not **also** involve the operation of my brain, and, however many life-support systems I may be plugged into, once my brain is dead I am, in a physical sense at least, no more.

If a person accepts that all physical processes are causally determined, and that all personal choices and moral decisions can be reduced to electrical impulses in the brain, then the whole of ethics is meaningless. Our apparent freedom is an illusion caused by our failure to monitor our brain activity.

A reductionist view also drains moral language of any valid meaning. A philosophical movement called Logical Positivism, which was influential in the early part of the twentieth century, took the view that statements had a valid meaning only if they were true by definition, or if they could be shown to be true by observation. So, for example, 'two plus two equals four' would make sense, because it is a matter of mathematical definition. 'There is a tree in the garden' would also mean something – that, if you were to look out into the garden, you would see a tree. But the statement 'it is wrong to kill' would not be a definition, nor could you find anything in the world 'out there' that could correspond to the word 'wrong'. On this test, morality is meaning-less, because it deals with choices and values, rather than with simple facts.

Therefore the only form of ethics for a reductionist is descriptive ethics, saying what in fact happens in different societies. As to whether any of these things are right or wrong, that remains meaningless.

In the next chapter we shall be looking at the meaning of moral language, and, of course, description of human behaviour is a valid use of language. For a reductionist, however, that is **the only** use of moral language, for it is the only thing for which there is external evidence.

Notice why it is important to think clearly about reductionist and determinist claims:

- A determinist says that all decisions are the result of prior factors. If determinism is true, we are not free to choose what to do. We therefore deserve neither praise nor blame for our actions. We do not have to **know** all the causes to take a determinist view – we just have to believe that there **are** sufficient causes.

- A reductionist claims that all talk about moral choice is really about electrical impulses in the brain. A reductionist therefore has little to say in moral debates.

- We cannot be told that we ought to do something, unless we can do it. That freedom is the basis of all moral argument.

—— HOW MUCH FREEDOM DOES —— MORALITY NEED?

Notice what moral language is **not** claiming:

- It does not claim that we are absolutely free.

- It does not claim that we are free to choose without any influence upon that choice (indeed, the more sensitive a person is, the more he or she is aware of such influences). It would be difficult to make sense of moral dilemmas unless there were come external constraints upon us: I struggle to know what is the right thing to do just because there are conflicting rules, loyalties or values, and I have to choose between them.

What it **does** claim is that:

- Whatever may happen in terms of the mechanical side of life, we experience ourselves as free agents who can make genuine choices.

- Even if I admit the existence of external moral pressure to conform to some rule, I am acting morally only if I am in a position to think about and either conform to, or reject, the pressures upon me.

- Other people, observing my behaviour, may come to conclusions about my personality and general attitude towards life. Having done so, they may predict accurately what I will do in any given circumstance. That element of prediction, however accurate, does not in itself prevent me from making a free choice.

—— FREEDOM AND THE STATE ——

In the discussion so far, we have been looking in a rather abstract way at whether or not a person is free to decide how to act. But in practical terms, even if we feel that we are free, we are actually constrained by the legal and social rules of the society within which we live.

If we are caught breaking a law, we are punished. If we are not caught, we may still feel guilty. Freedom is not simply a matter of biology, but of social and political life. If a person joins in a demonstration in favour of greater freedom, he or she is unlikely to be concerned about whether there can be a scientific explanation for each muscular action as he or she walks forward – but more likely to be campaigning for social or political freedom, and a restoration to the individual of choices presently prohibited by some authority.

But should every individual be free to choose exactly how he or she should live? Society needs to decide whether people in a particular country will drive on the right or the left; otherwise there will be chaos on the roads. Common sense dictates that an individual should not have the freedom to drive on the other side. But should everyone automatically have a right to take part in the democratic process to select a government? The answer to this is not so clear, because the results are less obvious.

Plato, for example, (in *The Republic* book IX) argued that most ordinary people did not have a strongly rational nature, and therefore needed to be constrained in what they did by being ruled by those who were naturally more rational. Philosophers alone, he thought, would have sufficient detachment to be able to legislate for the good of society as a whole.

In that book, Plato presents the different arguments in the form of a debate between individuals. One of these, Thrasymachus, argues that laws are always made in the interests of the ruling class, and Glaucon comments that basically everyone would like to act from purely selfish motives, although all would suffer as a result of the ensuing chaos. Both of these views of human and social motives find echoes throughout the history of ethics. If most people live selfishly, social anarchy may result, therefore, some argue, you must have some established principles of right and wrong, to which people are required to give their allegiance.

An Example:

Pope John Paul II issued a papal encyclical in September 1993 restating the Catholic position on birth control, homosexuality, pre-marital sex and other issues. Some of these will be examined later, but the fundamental point raised by the encyclical is one of freedom: should an individual be free to decide matters of personal morality for himself or herself? The answer given by the Catholic Church is that they should not; that divinely guided, the Church has an authority which takes precedence over the desires of individual members. In Catholic teaching a person is not free to decide the right or wrong of these major issues – that has already been settled. The only freedom is that of either obeying or rejecting the moral teachings.

As we come to examine the arguments about various ways of deciding just what it means to say that something is right or wrong, we need to keep in mind the exact nature of our freedom. We have to consider whether scientific prediction, and a full causal chain, are sufficient to justify the idea that we are not free.

Yet even if we accept the experience of freedom, we then need to ask of our freedom:

- Is it an absolute freedom, or one constrained by laws?

- What is the actual reason why I feel constrained by such laws (fear of punishment; social conditioning; genuine respect for the logic of the imposition of such laws)?

- Does the acceptance of social and legal restraints absolve me of responsibility for what I do (or don't do)?

A *situation*:

John Demjanjuk

In July 1993 an Israeli court found John Demjanjuk innocent of being 'Ivan the Terrible', a concentration camp guard who was reported to have taken a personal delight in the deaths of 900,000 Jews in the Treblinka death camp during the Second World War. His identity was not proved, and there was conflicting evidence. Although he may not have been Ivan the Terrible, it was clear that Demjanjuk had been captured by the Germans, and had worked for them.

His acquittal led to an outburst of anger in Israel. Many people felt that, even if his identity as that particular guard was not established, he must have done **something** worthy of punishment. One journalist wrote '... the judges failure to find a way to mark Demjanjuk for ever before the world as the criminal he certainly was, meant that morality was set aside'.

But our concern here is with freedom. So, in the light of the court's decision and the reaction to it in Israel, let us look at a couple of features of Demjanjuk's life and ask 'To what extent was he acting as a free man?' Here are some points raised at the time by Barbara Amiel, a British journalist:

'John Demjanjuk was 19 years old when he was pushed into Stalin's Red Army to fight the Nazis. His education had been rudimentary. His family had suffered desperately under Stalin's man-made famine that deliberately starved to death 20 million Ukrainians. When captured by the Nazis in 1942, it seems

---

Demjanjuk was offered a chance to work for them. What did he know of Nazi ideology? Auschwitz was in the Nazi mind, but had not yet been activated. Jews themselves did not believe in it. What would you do to get an extra crust of bread and live?'

Did he make a free choice to work for the Nazis? Was it the sort of freedom required to say that a person is guilty of war crimes? Should he, perhaps, have chosen death? Later, in America after the war, he had another 'choice':

'When Demjanjuk had the chance in the early 1950s to get out of the displaced persons camp in which he was, he lied to the American authorities. He did not mention that he had worked for the Nazis. To have mentioned it would have made him ineligible for an American visa and he would have been sent back to the USSR. To have told the truth in 1952 would have meant certain execution by Stalin.'

She mentions also those Jews in the death camps who were given food and a chance to live a little longer in exchange for cleaning out the gas chambers. In such an horrific situation, she asks what she would have done, and is grateful that she was never put to that test.

She then makes a point that is central to the issue of freedom and morality:

'How can you judge in freedom what a person does who exists in an unfree and indecent society?'

[Quotes taken from 'Judgments that are best left to God' article by Barbara Amiel, *The Sunday Times* August 8th 1993.]

The Demjanjuk case highlights a central point in all ethical discussion – 'To what extent are any of us free?' and 'To what extent are any of us able to judge the choices made by others, without experiencing directly the pressures and restriction on their freedom?'.

A SUMMARY

- Nobody is completely free.

- Everyone acts within physical, emotional, social, legal or political constraints.

- Such constraints still leave scope for freedom of the will.

- Determinism suggests that everything we do, and the choices we 'freely' make, are in fact determined by antecedent causes, our freedom is an illusion.

- A reductionist will go further, and see the very process of thought as 'nothing but' electrical and physical processes, for a reductionist, ethics is meaningless.

- We act according to the values and principles we hold. These may be given by the state. In this way, our actual freedom of action may be limited by laws, and our freedom of the will may be limited both by the unconscious acceptance of society's values.

- All moral choices therefore take place within a set of personal and social conditions. Ethical discussion may be abstract and general, but its application to life needs to be concrete and specific.

3

–WHAT DO WE MEAN?–

—— THREE KINDS OF LANGUAGE ——

To make moral statements, or to argue about them in ethical debate, we have to use language, and much of 20th century ethics has been concerned with the meaning of moral statements, and whether it is possible to show that they are either true or false. So once we have decided that we are free to make moral choices and to talk about them, we need to address the problem of the sort of language that we will be using to do so.

In ethics, there are three different kinds of language used. We need to distinguish them carefully, and know which we are using at any one time, if we are not to become confused.

DESCRIPTIVE ETHICS

This is the most straightforward form of ethics. It consists of the description of the way in which people live, and the moral choices they make. It simply presents facts. Here are some simple examples of descriptive ethics:

'Most car crime is carried out by young men in areas of high unemployment.'

The actual information may be correct or incorrect. It can be checked by referring to police records, and employment statistics.

But notice that the statement does not make any moral claim about youth and crime, nor does it say whether unemployment is a good or bad thing. It does not even make (although it may be taken to imply) a connection between crime and unemployment.

'Muslim men may marry up to four wives, provided that they are able to provide for them and treat them equally.'

Again, this makes no moral judgement, nor does it enquire whether it is possible to treat wives equally. It simply states the fact about what is permitted within a certain religious and cultural setting.

The danger with descriptive ethics is that it may imply moral judgements by the way in which information is presented, without actually explaining the basis on which those judgements are made.

NORMATIVE ETHICS

Ethics is concerned with ideas about what is right, about justice, about how people should live. It examines the choices people make and the values and reasoning that lie behind them. This is sometimes called 'substantive' or 'normative' ethics – and it is about the meaning and use of moral terms. Almost all moral argument, when it is concerned with the rights or wrongs of particular issues, is of this kind.

'It is always wrong to steal.'

This is a normative statement. It can be challenged by using another normative statement, e.g. 'No, I think it is right to steal on some occasions.' What you cannot do is challenge a normative statement by using a descriptive one. So a person who responds by saying 'But everyone around here steals if they get a chance' is not actually countering the claim that it is wrong to steal. Everyone may do something, but that does not make it right.

Descriptive ethics is about facts, normative ethics is about values. Both are needed, but it is essential to realise that you cannot argue directly from the one to the other, you cannot get an 'ought' from an 'is'.

META-ETHICS

It is also possible to stand back from moral statements and ask:

- 'What does it mean to say that something is right or wrong?'
- 'Are there any objective criteria by which I can assess moral statements?'
- 'What is moral language? Is it a statement about facts of any kind?'
- 'Does a moral statement simply express a person's wishes or hopes about what should happen?'
- 'In what sense can a moral statement be said to be either true or false?'

Questions like these are not concerned with the content of moral discourse, but with its meaning. Now this fits in very closely with much twentieth century philosophy, which has explored the nature of language and the way in which statements can be shown to be true or false. Looking at moral statements in this way is called 'Meta-ethics', and for some modern thinkers it is the most important aspect of ethics.

For a person coming to a study of ethics primarily in order to examine moral issues (rather than treating it as a branch of philosophy) there are two questions that might be asked of meta-ethical theories:

1 Does this theory ring true to my experience of making moral statements?

2 Does it actually help me to decide if something is right or wrong?

In other words, it may be correct in terms of linguistic analysis, but is it plausible and is it usable?

In this chapter we shall be looking at the meaning of some important moral words – some definitions of which were given by the ancient Greek philosophers, and which have been part of ethics ever since. But we shall also be looking at a number of meta-ethical theories. Although meta-ethics is a recent arrival on the philosophical scene, it is worth considering it now, so that, as we look at ethical theories of the past, we may assess them in terms of meaning, as well as in terms of their moral conclusions.

Notice that each kind of ethical language has its dangers:

- The danger of descriptive ethics is that facts will be mistaken for values.

- The danger of normative ethics is that – in arguing that something is right or wrong – one may end up preaching rather than informing, recommending one particular course of action rather than setting out all the possibilities, consequences and values, and then allowing a person to make an informed and thoughtful choice.

- The danger of meta-ethics is that one may become so obsessed with the issue of meaning, that it becomes impossible to offer any practical guidance for the difficult choices that people have to make.

——— DEFINING KEY WORDS ———

Moral language uses certain key words, without which normative ethics would not make sense. One of these is the word 'ought', expressing a sense of moral obligation. We shall see in Chapter 6 that this is fundamental to the experience of moral choice. Another is 'justice', examining the rights of individuals in society and the way in which they 'ought' to treat one another. Justice has been an important concept in social ethics since the ancient Greeks, and we shall look at it in Chapter 8, as part of our consideration of law and order.

The most basic word, however, is 'good'. An action is judged 'right' or 'wrong' depending upon whether or not it is a 'good' or 'bad' thing to do. Before we can talk about moral values we need to know what we mean by this term. Actions can't be right or wrong unless we know what we mean by goodness. But can it be defined?

You could try to define 'good' in absolute terms (that something is good in itself) or in relative terms (that it is good in its particular context). You can also define it in terms of what it can achieve – so an action is 'good' (and right) if the results of that action are 'good'. This would be a 'utilitarian' assessment, as we shall see later. But we are still using the word 'good' and are therefore no nearer a definition.

Aristotle defined as 'good' something which fulfilled its purpose. On this theory, a good knife is one that cuts well; a good plant is one that grows strong and healthy. This formed the basis of what is called the 'Natural Law' approach to ethics, which we shall examine in the next chapter. According to this, everything has a natural purpose in life, and actions are right or wrong depending on whether or not they contribute to the fulfilling of that purpose.

A religious believer may say that 'good' is what God approves, and take a particular revelation (e.g. the Bible) as the norm for understanding goodness. Another may take a particular experience, or the life of a religious leader, as the starting point for understanding the 'good' life. The meaning of the word good will therefore depend, in part, on the source of the values that are called 'good' – and that is not something on which everyone will automatically agree.

There are two important distinctions to be made when defining key words. Your definition can be **subjective** or **objective** (based on your own personal preferences, or based on certain external facts). It can also be **relative** or **absolute** (depending on individual circumstances, or something that should apply to all people at all times). Generally speaking, claims that are based on subjective preferences tend to be relative, and those that claim objectivity will also claim to be absolute.

As we go through the various ethical theories in this book we will find that there are many different aspects to the meaning of 'good'. But is it possible to say anything at all about it?

—————— SOME THEORIES ——————

We have already seen that much modern ethics is concerned with language – what moral language means, what it does, and how it may be verified. We shall now turn to look briefly at some modern theories about moral language. But first, before we can say anything about goodness, we have to decide whether or not we can actually know what goodness is:

INTUITIONISM

In 1903, G E Moore published *Principia Ethica*. In this he argued that goodness could not be defined, because it was unlike any other quality. In other words, if you try to say 'Something is good if...' you will never find a definition which does not reduce and limit the idea of goodness, and therefore make it inapplicable to other things.

He therefore came to the view that to say something is 'good' is rather like saying that it is 'yellow'. You cannot define a colour – you simply point to it and say 'That is what I mean by yellow.'. Try defining yellow for the benefit of someone who has never seen that colour – it cannot be done!

We know that something is 'good' by intuition – it is self-evident. You can define an action as being 'right' if it leads to a 'good' result. You can argue rationally about many moral problems, deciding which of various options will lead to the 'good', but you cannot define that basic idea in itself.

> 'Everyone does in fact understand the question "Is this good?". When he thinks of it, his state of mind is different from what it would be, were he asked "Is this pleasant, or desired, or approved?". It has a distinct meaning for him, even though he may not recognise in what respect it is distinct. Whenever he thinks of "intrinsic value" or "intrinsic worth", or says that a thing "ought to exist", he has before his mind the unique object – the unique property of things – which I mean by "good".'
>
> Moore, G E, *Principia Ethica,* Chapter 1, 1903

This theory is called 'intuitionism'. It was later developed particularly by W D Ross (in *The Right and the Good* 1930, and *Foundations of Ethics* 1939) and by H A Prichard (*Moral Obligation* 1937). Prichard argued, for example, that the idea of 'duty' was not definable. Our obligations to other people are self-evident.

Now there would seem to be a major objection to intuitionism. If what is good, and my duty, are self-evident, how is it that I can find myself in a quandary? Life is seldom straightforward, and I may find myself at a loss to know what I should do. Indeed, if people were never uncertain about what they should do, there would be no ethical debate at all! Ross overcame this difficulty by suggesting that I know what my duty is, but that sometimes that duty conflicts with some other, and a choice therefore has to be made. Ethical dilemmas are therefore the result of such conflicting duties. Even so, it would seem that there are times when people do not know what is right, and in a multi-cultural environment, where there is no single ethical tradition, people may not have clear intuitions about such matters.

A *situation*:

'A "light smacking" was sometimes the best way to control a child, a professor of psychology told a court yesterday.

A modern theory suggested children had no natural sense of what is right and what is wrong, said Prof Richard Lynn of the University of Ulster. "That sense has to be learned in early and middle childhood," he told Sutton magistrates.

"For some children physical discipline is an important part of that process. From time to time the most effective way of controlling a child is a light smack."

(From an article by Richard Spencer, *The Daily Telegraph* July 7th 1993)

- If this is so, at what point does a person develop an innate sense of what is right?

- And how can an adult tell if this apparently self-evident

> sense of right and wrong is not just the product of early
> training, now permanently enshrined in the unconscious?

In practical terms, Moore accepted that one might judge an action according to its predicted results – trying to do what maximises the good in the world. He differs from utilitarians (see Chapter 5) in that he will not allow that this assessment of results to *define* what is meant by 'good'.

EMOTIVISM (THE 'BOO!', 'HURRAY!' THEORY)

In the early part of the twentieth century there developed an approach to language which is generally known as 'Logical Positivism'. It was an attempt to break down language into its simplest components and examine their meaning. This movement is represented by the early work of Wittgenstein (*Tractatus Logico Philosophicus*) by the Vienna Circle of philosophers (including, for example, Carnap and Schlick) and, particularly influential in Britain, by A J Ayer's book *Language Truth and Logic*, 1936.

The details of this approach to linguistic philosophy need not detain us, except to say that it held that all meaningful propositions could be divided into two categories – tautologies and empirical statements of fact. The former were true by definition (e.g. the statements of mathematics) and the latter by observation. If a statement was not a tautology, and could not be shown to relate to externally perceived facts, then it was said to be meaningless. Now, on this basis, moral statements are meaningless, as they are neither statements of fact nor definitions. So if moral statements are not statements of fact or tautologies, what are they?

Ayer distinguished four different kinds of ethical statements:

> 'There are, first of all, propositions which express definitions of ethical terms, or judgements about the legitimacy or possibility of certain definitions. Secondly, there are propositions describing the phenomena of moral experience, and their causes. Thirdly, there are exhortations to moral virtue. And, lastly, there are actual ethical judge-

ments ... In fact, it is easy to see that only the first of our four classes, namely that which comprises the propositions relating to the definitions of ethical terms, can be said to constitute ethical philosophy. The propositions which describe the phenomena of moral experience, and their causes, must be assigned to the science of psychology, or sociology. The exhortations to moral virtue are not propositions at all, but ejaculations or commands which are designed to provoke the reader to action of a certain sort. Accordingly, they do not belong to any branch of philosophy or science. As for the expressions of ethical judgments, we have not yet determined how they should be classified. But inasmuch as they are certainly neither definitions nor comments upon definitions, nor quotations, we may say decisively that they do not belong to ethical philosophy. A strictly philosophical treatise on ethics should therefore make no ethical pronouncements.'

One response to this challenge is Emotivism, and may be represented here by C L Stevenson's theory in *Ethics and Language*, 1947. A J Ayer had argued that moral judgements expressed the feelings of the speaker, and of the members of the Vienna Circle, Carnap thought that moral statements were really commands (if I say 'This is the right thing to do' I really mean 'Do this!') and Schlick thought that they were rules. Bertrand Russell argued that differences in values (and therefore differences in the moral statements that are based on them) are not a matter of facts, but of taste.

Once you strip the supposed facts away from moral statements, they are revealed for what they really are, expressions of a person's own preferences and emotions. To say that something is wrong is really just another way of saying that I don't approve of it. This is the main feature of Stevenson's theory. He is less concerned with what moral statements mean in themselves, and more concerned with what they are *for*. Moral statements express the feelings of the speaker, and intend to influence the feelings of the hearer. A statement has an emotive meaning if it is intended to produce a response in the person who hears it. To say that something is 'good' means that you should approve of it.

There are two main criticisms of this approach. One (e.g. given by G J Warnock in *Contemporary Moral Philosophy*) is that a moral argument is not really judged according to the response it evokes, but on whether its claims are valid. Moral attitudes are not just about emotions, but are capable of being discussed rationally.

A second (given by Bernard Mayo in *The Philosophy of Right and Wrong* 1986) is that when you claim something is right or wrong, you are making a policy statement. You would be expected to take the same position in a similar situation; but this is not the case with emotions, which may vary. If I claim that my moral judgements are universal (I say what ought to apply to everyone) that cannot be based on a simple matter of feeling, for I can't say what everyone else should feel, nor can I know what I will feel on other occasions.

To put it crudely, the Emotive Theory reduces morality to a set of cheers or boos, sounded off in response to experiences that are liked or disliked. Now some people may indeed make moral statements on that basis, but it does not seem to be an adequate account of all the moral arguments that have taken place over the centuries, nor does it do justice to the rational character of human thought in this area of life. We may sometimes act out of impulse or simple feeling, but we often think things through and act rationally, and this should be the subject of moral discussion.

PRESCRIPTIVISM

Whereas the emotivist asks what sort of effect a moral statement aims to have, a prescriptivist is more concerned about what is happening when someone actually makes a moral statement. R M Hare (in *The Language of Morals* 1952 and *Freedom and Reason* 1963) is the best known representative of this approach. He asks about what a moral statement is meant to *do,* and concludes that a moral statement is 'prescribing' a course of action – actually recommending that something should be done, rather than just expressing the feelings of the speaker.

This may sound similar in practice to a command, but there is a difference. If I see someone about to steal a car and I shout out 'Stop that!' I am referring to that single incident. I am not suggesting that stopping doing things is a general principle on which I expect the person to base his life! On the other hand, if I say 'It is wrong to steal!' I am giving a piece of advice that can apply to future situations as well.

Nevertheless, prescribing and giving commands have something important in common. They both relate the content of what is said directly to the response that saying it is intended to have. Now this is certainly true of all commands, but is it true of all moral statements? I may discuss moral issues related to something which happened in the past. I may say, for example, that I believe the extermination of millions of Jews and others under the Nazi regime was absolutely wrong. That is a moral statement. But it is not directly suggesting that anyone with whom I am discussing that issue is actually in a position to respond to it in practical terms. I am not recommending a course of action. I am merely commenting on the way in which a certain action conforms to or goes against fundamental values that I hold.

A simple prescriptivist view might therefore need to be qualified by saying that a moral statement prescribes that, in certain circumstances, I believe that a particular action is the right one.

An important point made by Hare is that moral statements should be universalisable. We shall consider this again in Chapter 6, when we look at the philosopher Kant. For now we need note only that this underlines the distinction between a command and a prescriptive statement. The prescriptive statement is making a general point – one that could be applied to situations in the past and the future, and to other people, as well as to the person to whom it is addressed.

NATURALISM AND METAPHYSICAL ETHICS

Reading Plato's *Republic*, or Aristotle's *Ethics*, we get the very definite idea that, in spite of the various views that are examined, there is ultimately a rational basis for the idea of goodness and justice – arising from the nature of human life, or the needs of a society to organise itself in a harmonious way.

The implication of this is that there is an objective basis for ethics.

On the other hand, some of the theories put forward in this chapter may suggest that there is no objective truth in ethics, but that everything centres on the wishes or feelings of the person who makes the moral statement. This 'ethical subjectivism' may seem appropriate for a society that has no single religious, social, political or cultural base – for people differ from one another so greatly that it is unlikely that they would share the same values, or choose to act in the same way.

On the other hand, when it comes to moral issues, people try to persuade others about how they should behave. They argue as though there were some objective truth about which different people could agree. Indeed, if every moral choice is right or wrong depending on personal and individual tastes, there would seem little point in discussing moral issues at all.

This situation gives rise to two other theories about ethical language. 'Naturalistic Ethics' is the term used for the attempt to explain a set of moral terms from the facts of human life. It is the positive side of what G E Moore criticised as the 'naturalistic fallacy', the attempt to derive an 'ought' from an 'is'. To be fair, those who propose a modern naturalistic ethic (e.g. Richard Norman in *The Moral Philosophers* 1983) do so on the basis of observed social relationships and in a way that gets round the simple application of Moore's criticism. But naturalistic ethics still seems to 'reduce' moral language – to make it something else: pieces of social information.

By contrast, Metaphysical Ethics insists that morality should be valued in itself, and should be related to our understanding of the world and of our place within it. It points out that moral choices are related to our general understanding of life, and the value that we find in it: in other words, to our 'metaphysics'.

A SUMMARY OF THESE THEORIES

- Intuitionism – one just instinctively knows when something is right!

- Emotivism – one uses moral statements to express feelings, and influence the feelings of others.

- Prescriptivism – one uses moral statements to 'prescribe' a general course of action.

- Naturalism – relating moral statements to particular features of the world and of social relationships.

- Metaphysical Ethics – relating moral statements to a general understanding of the world, its meaning and its values.

Now it is clear that when we use moral language we may be doing a combination of some or all of these things. We may speak about something being good without knowing how to define what we mean by that word. We may speak out because we want to express our emotions. We may want to recommend a course of action. We may also feel convinced that there are objective grounds for saying that something is right or wrong.

The important thing is to be aware of all these theories of 'meta-ethics' so that we recognise the basis upon which we are using moral language, and thus save a great deal of misunderstanding and arguing at cross purposes. It is also important as we turn to some important theories in the history of ethics, to recognise the bases that those thinkers are using.

It will be clear from looking at the meta-ethical theories above that we can take either a subjective approach to ethics (it expresses my feelings, my intuitions about what is right, or my prescribed course of action), or an objective approach (there are features of the world and of human beings that make this particular action right and that one wrong).

In general, the more subjective approaches will produce criteria which are personal and individual. The more objective ones will produce criteria which are able to be applied universally.

If we are free to choose what to do, and we are aware of the problems of using moral language, the next question we need to ask is:

'Shall I act on personal impulse and intuition, or is there any objective guidance which can help me decide what is the right thing for me to do?'

In the chapters that follow we shall be looking at a variety of bases people have used for their ethical statements:

- based on what is 'natural', and a rational understanding of nature;

- based on results;

- based on a sense of moral duty.

4

—— IS IT NATURAL? ——

So far we have looked at whether or not we are free to decide how to act, and what it means to make a moral statement. But moral statements, even if they are expressing a personal preference or recommending a course of action, make claims about 'right' and 'wrong'. We saw in Chapter 1 that it is impossible to decide moral issues simply by checking facts. Is there any other rational or objective basis upon which you can argue that something is 'right' or 'wrong'?

In the chapters that follow we shall be looking at some attempts to find a basis for moral judgements, to justify them in terms of the expected results of an action, or the experience of a sense of 'ought', or the desire for personal growth, or the needs of society. But first we shall examine a theory which claims that everything is created to a particular design and for a particular purpose, and that fulfilling that purpose is what is 'good' to which everything aims. It is called the theory of 'natural law'.

'Natural law', as an ethical theory, was developed by Thomas Aquinas in the 13th century, and it became a central feature of Catholic moral thinking. To find its roots, however, we need to go back to the 4th century BCE and the philosophy of Aristotle.

— DOES IT HAVE A 'FINAL CAUSE'? —

Aristotle distinguished between 'efficient causes' and 'final causes': an efficient cause is what gets things done, a final cause is the end product. A child grows up to be an adult. Aristotle would say that an 'efficient cause' of the child's growth is food and drink, but the 'final cause' is the adult into which the child is growing. Similarly, if I take a piece of wood and carve it into a statue, the efficient cause is the knife that I use, but the final cause is the image that I seek to create.

On this theory, everything, both every object and every action, has some final meaning and purpose (its 'final cause') and this is what determines its 'good'. If we understand what that 'good' is, we will know what we need to do in order to achieve it. There are other important themes in Aristotle's ethics, including the idea of achieving a balance between the extremes of excess and deficiency, but the 'natural law' theory is based on this idea of final causes and the corresponding 'good' towards which all things are designed to work.

Aquinas used this idea to argue that the world was created by God, and that everything should therefore have God's ultimate purpose as its final 'end' or 'good'. Each individual thing had a design and a purpose (in other words, its 'final cause') and to understand God's will for it, and therefore what is 'right' for it, you only have to look at the purpose for which it has been made.

A good knife is one that cuts well: that's what it's designed to do. But how do you decide what is a good human life?

Aquinas argued that everything had its proper 'act' and 'end', and that this was given as part of God's providential ordering of the world. But humankind was special in that it was given reason and freedom. Humans could therefore understand and choose to follow their final good. This he called 'natural law' – the rational understanding and following of God's final purpose.

Let us take an example which has been important within Catholic moral thought:

Example:

Consider the act of heterosexual intercourse. (Sadly, we need to consider its 'final cause', although its 'efficient causes' tend to be more entertaining.)

- Its natural purpose is to fertilise an egg, which in turn will be nurtured within a womb to produce another human being. This process will help maintain the human species.

- Given the physical contortions involved, it is difficult to imagine how copulation could occur by random chance in the course of normal social life! Sexual attraction and arousal is therefore the means that nature has supplied for achieving this particular end.

- Sexual arousal and the act of penetration are therefore the 'efficient cause', whilst the production of a new human being is the 'final cause' of the sexual act.

If it is the 'final cause' that determines if something is right or wrong, then strictly speaking, in terms of sex:

- Intercourse between members of the same sex is wrong (because it cannot result in conception);

- Intercourse with those who are outside the age range for child bearing is wrong (for the same reason);

- Anal and oral intercourse and masturbation are wrong (for the same reason);

- Any attempt to frustrate the process of conception is wrong, because it tries to separate off the sexual act from its natural purpose.

In traditional Catholic teaching it is therefore wrong to practise contraception. Each sexual act should include the possibility of conception.

Pope Paul VI's encyclical letter Humanae Vitae (1968) expresses it in this way:

'The Church... in urging men to the observance of the precepts of the natural law, which it interprets by its constant doctrine, teaches as absolutely required that any use whatsoever of marriage must retain its natural potential to procreate human life.'

Sex within the 'safe period' of the woman's ovulatory cycle is generally permitted in Catholic moral teaching because the failure to conceive in this situation is part of nature's limitation, rather than the result of a direct attempt to do something unnatural. The same applies to those who are past child bearing age, on the grounds that, by a miracle, conception might take place.

This example shows that 'natural law', unlike most other theories we shall be considering, gives the possibility of producing a clearly defined rule which can then be applied universally. An action is right or wrong in itself, without reference to all its possible consequences (e.g. an act of sex might result in the birth of a child who grows up to be a mass murderer, but that does not make the sexual act morally wrong, only regrettable!).

You may not always know what the results of your actions will be. You are therefore only responsible for the immediate consequences of your action, not for any secondary and unintended effects. This is sometimes called 'the law of double effect'. It can be a surprisingly useful theory for those who wish to practise contraception without going against 'natural law', because if a woman suffers from painful or irregular periods, a doctor may prescribe 'contraceptive' pills in order to regulate her cycle. The fact that the hormone in the pills acts as a contraceptive is a secondary effect, and is not the intention of the original prescription. 'Natural law' morality is maintained: the doctor is right in his prescription, because it has the intended effect of regulating the cycle and relieving discomfort, the woman is right in having sex while taking the pill, because the pill is not an deliberate attempt to frustrate conception.

This is not offered as a cynical attempt to undermine 'natural law', but to illustrate the problem of trying to find a single objective rule to cover a situation which may have many complex layers of meaning and intention. Natural law requires an 'act analysis' approach to moral argument, i.e. it breaks the situation down into the various acts involved and tries to establish the absolute morality of each. In practice, a couple may have sex for many different physical and emotional reasons, and 'natural law' does not allow for these to be taken into account.

By contrast, the approach to the issue of contraception taken by other religious groups, along with most secular moral thinkers, is based on the expected results. It takes into account factors like the ability of the couple to provide for any children they may conceive. Globally, contraception may be promoted because of population problems in areas of poverty – again, an argument based on results. Because there are many factors to be weighed, the decision about contraception is generally left to the conscience of the individuals concerned.

——— SOME FEATURES OF ———
'NATURAL LAW'

- The term 'natural law' can be used simply to refer to the laws of nature. In this sense, natural law is the basis of all science. It is the result of observing what happens in nature.

- As traditionally presented, the 'natural law' theory of ethics is based on the religious idea of a God who creates everything with a particular purpose and end in mind. People are therefore required to understand that end and act accordingly, if they are to do what is right.

- 'Natural law' can be examined quite apart from its religious interpretation, as a rational theory relating behaviour to the basic features of human life, its place within the world, and the basic requirements for its survival.

- It has the advantage that, once a 'final cause' is established, it may be applied to all people at all times. A natural law theory of sex, therefore, will take little account of prevailing society – it is about sperm and egg, not about lifestyle.

- It is not based on personal preferences, nor of guessing what the results of an action might be in terms of the happiness or otherwise of those involved – it is simply based on an examination of what is 'natural'. Potentially, it is a very 'clear cut' ethical theory.

Natural law supports other general views of moral behaviour. Aquinas (in *Summa Theologica*) presented the four cardinal virtues – prudence, justice, fortitude and temperance (which had been used as a basis for morality by the Stoics) -as fundamental qualities of the moral life. The opposite to these virtues are the seven capital vices (often called the 'seven deadly sins'), which are pride, avarice, lust, envy, gluttony, anger and sloth. From a traditional standpoint of belief in God, one might say that the former allow a human being to fulfil his or her potential as a human being as intended by God, whereas the latter frustrate that intention, and therefore go against God's will.

But the issue of what is 'natural' is wider than Aquinas' theory, for 'natural law' is essentially about finding the rational principles upon which the world is made and which may therefore guide action. But many actions that are called 'natural' are destructive, and against any rational principles. So there are further questions to be asked:

— HOW DO YOU DECIDE WHAT IS — 'NATURAL'?

Science builds up laws based on observation. If something is observed that does not fit in with an established law, then either the observation is wrong, or there is another as yet unknown law which, in this particular case, has unexpectedly come into operation. Our understanding of the way in which nature works is therefore constantly being modified.

If this also applies to 'natural law' as an ethical theory, then we cannot establish fixed criteria for right and wrong – which was the aim of Aquinas and others who followed this line of thought – because our concept of what is natural, and therefore of 'final causes' will always be open to modification.

Natural law is about what life should be like, given a rational and purposeful creation, but that may not be what life is actually like.

Examples:

It is natural for someone who is seriously ill to die.

- Does that mean that one should not interfere with the natural course of a disease by giving medicine?

In the natural world, the strongest animals often mate with as many sexual partners as they can, fighting off weaker rivals.

- Should there be selective breeding amongst humans? Is monogamy unnatural?

These examples suggest that there is no easy way to establish the 'final cause' that will enable us to say with certainty that we know exactly what every thing or action is for, what part it has to play in an overall purposeful scheme of the universe.

The idea that the universe as a whole has a purpose and direction, and that it (and everything in it) has been created for a specific reason, is not a matter of scientific argument, but of religious belief. Those without such belief will not necessarily see a rationally justified 'final cause'. Indeed, one of the main arguments against belief in God has been the apparent pointlessness of suffering. Once pointlessness replaces purpose as a general view of the natural world, then the 'natural law' argument starts to break down.

We saw in Chapter 3 that moral statements cannot be established by the observation of facts, and that you cannot argue from something that 'is' the case to something that 'ought' to be the case. This is really a matter of linguistic philosophy rather than ethics, but it is relevant to any argument which seeks to take what is perceived in nature as a basis for moral action.

When you record facts, you do just that, you show what has happened and what is happening now. Facts are neutral in terms of ethics. Once you make a moral statement, you bring in your values and wishes, you recommend that something should be done, or you express your own feelings. These things are over and above the facts to which they are applied.

Now the 'natural law' argument seems at first sight to get round this. It tries to argue from something that 'is' (the nature of the world) to something that 'ought' to be done. In practice, however, it does so because it uses two ideas which do not come from the facts about the world. The first of these is human freedom (see Chapter 2) and the second is belief in a creator God who guarantees that things do have a purpose which suits their nature, and to which they can respond in a positive and creative way.

There are other ways of trying to link 'ought' and 'is'. In Eastern religious thought the idea of karma – that actions have consequences that cumulatively influence the future – relates the state of the world to moral choices. But this gives only a 'hypothetical' command (in other words, one that says 'If you want to achieve X, then you must do Y') not an absolute moral command. To get an absolute command (or 'categorical imperative', as we shall see later) you have to presuppose someone who gives the command. Within the natural law theory, that 'someone' is God.

—— APPLYING 'NATURAL LAW' ——

It is one thing to have universal principles, another to apply them to individual cases. This is often referred to as a 'deductive' method of moral argument – one that starts with general rules and then deduces the morality of a particular situation from them. This process may also be called 'casuistry'. Often regarded as a pejorative term (implying that the principle is applied in an unfeeling, contrived, or irrelevant way), the process is part of a common sense approach to ethics. We have already looked at the 'natural law' view of sex and contraception, so let us continue that theme.

An example:

Two adults of the same sex are attracted to one another. They wish to express that attraction physically, to live together with the same legal and social support that they would receive as a heterosexual couple, to adopt children, and to bring them up in a family home. Is what they wish to do morally right?

- Homosexual acts between consenting male adults are legal in many countries, although the age of consent varies from country to country. In some Muslim countries, following strict Shari'ah laws, homosexuality is punishable by death. By contrast, in Classical Greece, homosexual love was widely practised, and socially acceptable. There is therefore no universally held view about homosexuality and its place in society.

- Since homosexuality involves what used to be called 'unnatural acts', it is a particularly suitable situation against which to test 'natural law' as an ethical theory.

This is how a 'natural law' argument might view that homosexual partnership:

- According to Natural Law, the purpose of sex is procreation. Since homosexual acts cannot lead to conception, they are 'unnatural' and therefore wrong.

- On this basis, heterosexual acts within a stable relationship (i.e. one that will enable children to be nurtured – often considered within 'natural law' arguments to imply marriage) or celibacy are the only two morally acceptable sexual choices that a person can make.

- Because of this, there is no moral objection in natural law to the couple living together, or feeling attracted towards one another. The only objection is to any physical sexual acts that may take place between them.

- Because they cannot form a 'natural' family group, homosexual couples should not be allowed to adopt children, who 'naturally' thrive only with the benefit of both 'mother' and 'father' role models.

Against this line of argument:

- One might argue that the presence of sexual organs in a human being implies that he or she is designed for sexual activity and the conception of children – in which case, celibacy is as unnatural as homosexuality, since it is a denial of the complete natural function of procreation. If this is established, then it is illogical to accept a celibate partnership between those who are sexually attracted.

- Some people are naturally attracted by members of the same sex. They do not experience their feelings as 'unnatural', but as completely natural. Any difficulties they experience are the result of social conditioning, not nature.

- Sexuality can be said to achieve three ends:

  1. physical pleasure

  2. the deepening of a relationship

  3. the conception of children.

  Of which only the third is precluded by homosexual relationships. But is not the search for pleasure and for deep relationships as 'natural' as the conception of children? If a marriage is known to be infertile, are heterosexual acts between its partners therefore immoral? – which would be the case if the absence of the possibility of conception makes sex 'wrong' because it is 'unnatural'.

- Marriage is a social function, and promiscuity can be practised equally by homosexuals and heterosexuals. The fact that homosexual couples cannot marry does not preclude deep and permanent relationships.

- If a homosexual couple form a stable relationship, they

> may be able to offer children a home that is, at the very least, as valuable to their upbringing as one in which there is either a single parent, or a heterosexual couple with a bad relationship.

In pointing out some of the ways in which the 'natural law' view of the homosexual couple's situation might be challenged, it is not intended to undermine the principle of 'natural law' as such, but to show that there are some areas of morality – particularly where relationships are concerned – where it is difficult to consider morality mainly in terms of specific actions.

RAPE

The sexual urge is probably the strongest of all human inclinations, and it is 'natural' – both in the sense that it fits in with what people would do in a natural state, unchecked by laws, and also because (through its functions of continuing the species) it has a place within 'natural law' scheme of morality.

Although social customs and laws vary from one country to another, heterosexual intercourse is generally legal provided:

- the partners are over the age of consent

- consent is freely given

- it does not cause public nuisance (e.g. it should be done in private)

Rape is the term used for an act of sexual intercourse where consent is not given, or where a partner is below the age at which valid consent can be given (statutory rape). It is the violation of one person by another, as opposed to legal sexual intercourse, which is enjoyed (hopefully) by mutual agreement. But once we start to ask about what is natural, there are many issues to be considered:

- According to natural law, every act of intercourse should be open to the possibility of conception, and should (on a strict interpretation) have that as its 'end'. Does this mean that the forcible act of intercourse imposed by a husband upon a wife in order to conceive a child (assuming that the wife does not want to conceive) is therefore right?

- Is marital rape possible, or does marriage imply acceptance of sexual intercourse under all conditions? Is there a point at which it is 'natural' for one or other partner to refuse to have sex?

- In the case of the rape of a stranger, it is assumed that the person committing the rape is sexually attracted by the person raped. (In this sense, the act is 'natural'.) If the person raped actually dresses in a way that is sexually provocative, or behaves in a provocative manner, can he or she be considered to have contributed to that act or rape, by deliberately behaving in a way that invites sexual attention? Is it 'natural' to want to look sexy? If so, can one then argue that it is wrong for a person to respond to that implied sexual invitation?

A situation:

Date rape

Two students attend a dance, and both become drunk. They return at the end of the evening to the girl's room and sexual intercourse takes place. The following day, realising what has happened, the girl complains that she has been raped. In defence, her partner argues that they were both drunk at the time, and that the girl was a willing partner in the sexual act, and was not subject in any way to force.

- If there are no strict social rules (e.g. if it is believed that other students in a similar situation would willingly take part in sex), does acceptance of a situation (returning to her room) imply consent?

- Can rape be retrospectively applied to an unwise sexual act?

- How specific does consent have to be? Does it have to include verbal agreement, or can it be intuited?

- 'Date rape' is a feature of social ambiguity. Two people go

---

out together, each expecting something rather different of the other. Is it reasonable to separate out the act of intercourse (which gives rise to the claim that rape has taken place) from the rest of the social situation?

- Does it make any moral sense, in the case of date rape, to ask about what is 'natural' as opposed to what is agreed by written, verbal or implied contract?

This issue of date rape highlights the difference between 'natural law', what is 'natural' and what is socially acceptable. It is an area where legislation seems most difficult to frame, simply because it is such a 'natural' situation, open to the personal interpretation of the parties involved.

— ARE WE NATURALLY GOOD OR — BAD?

The philosopher Thomas Hobbes (1588-1679), in his book *Leviathan*, saw the life of man in a natural state as 'solitary, poor, nasty, brutish and short'. He took the view that, left to their own devices, people are naturally greedy. They want freedom, but also power (which included riches, reputation, success, nobility and eloquence – all that might give one person an advantage over others), and the inevitable result of this is that they would struggle against one another in order to gain it. In such a society, everyone is judged by his or her power:

> 'The *value*, or WORTH of a man, is as of all other things, his price; that is to say, so much as would be given for the use of his power: and therefore is not absolute, but a thing dependent on the need and judgement of another.'

Unbridled competition, allied to seeing everyone in terms of his or her power, may lead to social anarchy. Hobbes therefore argued that it was in the self interest of all for people to set aside their claim to total power, in order that they might live peacefully with others, for otherwise there will be constant danger of losing everything. In effect, he came down to a form of the 'golden rule' – do as you would be done to. He applied reason to human society, pointing out what was needed for society to function – but recognised that, without that reason, people would be in a state of self-destructive greed and anarchy.

Such anarchy would not have been tolerated for long by Niccolo Machiavelli (1469-1527), who (in *The Prince*) argues that a ruler must know how to use his power and needs be feared as well as respected by his people. His views on political power, and the measures that a person should be prepared to employ in order to gain and maintain it, suggest that in a natural state humankind is ruthless and competitive. Both Hobbes and Machiavelli see natural life as essentially a struggle for power and survival.

By contrast, Jean-Jacques Rousseau (1712-1778) thought that people were born essentially good, as was everything that came directly from nature. He argued that, if the conditions are right, people will flourish and be morally good. Human nature is fine in itself, the trouble is with the way in which society is organised. Another example of this positive attitude to the natural is Henry David Thoreau (1817-1862). In *Walden, or Life in the Woods*, he saw God within all nature, and everything is therefore inherently good. He argued that people spent too much time worrying about earning a living, and seeking for things they do not really need – leading lives of 'quiet desperation'. By contrast, he sought a far simpler and more natural way of living.

We shall be looking at these thinkers again later. For now we need only recognise that human life is complex, and it is seldom possible to see what it would be like without the constraints of society. Opinion is divided:

- Are human beings fundamentally ruthless and savage, restrained and tamed by society, but liable at times to revert to their 'natural' behaviour?

- Or are human beings fundamentally good and caring, made antisocial and brutalised by society, but, given the right environment, capable of reverting to their gentler nature?

Points for reflection:

- Looking at the items in any newspaper (or those given at the end of Chapter 1) consider if, on the basis of the situations outlined in it, you consider humankind to be more 'Hobbes' or more 'Rousseau' (i.e. to use an extreme form – more 'savages tamed by society' or more 'angels corrupted by society'):

- What do these views suggest about punishment and reform?

- Should society have more rules or less?

- Should morality be left to the conscience of the individual, or be imposed by society?

- Aristotle saw reason as the distinctive human quality? Was he right?

- John Stuart Mill (whose ethics we shall look at in Chapter 5), pointed out that most of the things people are punished for doing (e.g. murder, rape) are a common occurrence in nature. Should ethics be seen therefore as a distinctively human step away from the natural order?

- Watch a cat 'play' with a mouse.

So far in this chapter we have moved from a formal and rational view of nature – the 'natural law' argument of Aquinas and others – to a brief look at the more general question of 'naturalism' in ethics. But there are two other issues related to this. The first is the question of evolution, and whether it offers a better basis for morality than a static view of nature. The second is whether the whole idea of getting general rules and applying them to individual cases is wrong, and morality should be based on an individual's response to a particular situation.

— EVOLUTION, CHANGE AND THE — NATURAL LAW

If the whole world is in a state of constant change; if galaxies are moving outwards towards an unknown future; if stars are born and die, and planets spinning around them are vulnerable to their death and many other cosmic accidents; if life on planet Earth is a recent phenomenon and subject to a process of evolution – how can anything have a fixed purpose or goal?

Darwin's theory of natural selection is not part of ethics. It is a scientific theory, based on the observation of species. It argues that those best adapted to their environment will prosper and multiply. Species that fail to adapt will eventually decline and vanish. It does not say that this ought to happen, it just observes life and tries to provide a theory to explain it.

It is tempting, however, to create a morality based on evolution. Henri Bergson (1859-1941) in *Creative Evolution,* felt that you should act in a way that enables you follow the stream of evolutionary life in the direction of the future – that you should do nothing to impede the progress of evolution. Herbert Spencer, in *The Principles of Ethics*, came to the view that the good is what gives pleasure. But he also considered 'the survival of the fittest' and was prepared to say that misfits, weaklings or those who are stupid should be left to their fate, and should not be allowed to impede the rise and progress of those who are more able.

In a way (although he did not link it specifically with evolution) this reflects the attitude of Friedrich Nietzsche (see Chapter 7) who spoke of slave morality and master morality, and felt that Christianity and democracy were holding back human progress by allowing too much consideration to be given to the weak at the expense of the strong, encouraging the attitude of 'slaves' rather than that of the 'masters'.

In Chapter 7, we shall look at personal development as a basis for ethics, but notice how very different this is in its approach from 'natural law'. In 'natural law' you look at particular actions and judge if they, in themselves, are right or wrong. Any theory of personal or global development – of evolution, in other words — looks at each decision and action in the light of the direction of evolution and change. What will this action allow me to become? What effect will this action have on the future of humankind? Such ethics is dynamic and forward looking – and it is based on results, not on the intrinsic value of an individual action.

─────── SITUATION ETHICS ───────

The natural law approach to ethics formulates rules and then applies them to individual situations. But is it right to apply rules in this way? Is not every situation unique?

In the 1960s, largely as a reaction against what he saw as a paternalistic and imposed morality of traditional Christianity, Joseph Fletcher developed 'Situation Ethics'.

He argued against the deductive method of ethics (in which you start with a rule or principle, and then apply it to various particular cases), and suggested that the individual situation should be paramount. He believed that there should be a single moral principle – that you should do whatever is the most loving thing. Ethical rules were of secondary importance – they might guide a person, but should not dictate right and wrong.

The requirement to do the most loving thing is not a rule or law – it does not say **what** you should do in any particular situation – it merely gives a motive and attitude which can inform moral choice. Of course, a person may act foolishly out of love, with disastrous consequences – but nevertheless, from a strictly situationist ethical perspective – it is still morally right.

Following 'Situation Ethics' you take each individual situation and judge it by what love requires, and if you have to break some conventional moral rule in the process, you are morally right to do so.

Other writers from the same period took a position half way between this radical 'situation' approach and the conventional application of rules. Paul Tillich (in *Morality and Beyond* 1963), pointed out that, if there were no rules, then everyone would have to work out what he or she should do on every individual occasion. This, he argued, was too much to expect. There should be rules to help people decide what love might require of them in any given situation.

─────────── TWO ISSUES ───────────

In order to draw together some of the questions that have been explored in this chapter, we shall look at two moral issues. The first - artificial methods of helping human fertility - involves the ethics of 'natural law', set in the context of developments in medicine, and in a situation where people are emotionally involved. The second - euthanasia - probes the balance between general rules and the demands of love in particular situations.

ARTIFICIAL METHODS OF CONCEPTION?

The situation:

Statistics vary, but around 10 per cent of heterosexual partnerships are naturally infertile. Of these, the infertility is due to the woman in about 85% of cases.

The possibilities for overcoming this are:

1. If it is not possible for the couple to conceive through copulation, the male partner's semen may be used for artificial insemination: called AIH. (Artificial Insemination – Husband).

2. If the male partner is infertile, the couple could use semen from a donor: called AID. (Artificial Insemination – Donor).

3. If the woman cannot produce a viable ovum, this can be supplied by a donor, fertilised using the partner's semen, and then implanted in the womb.

4. Where neither ovum nor semen are viable, both can be donated, brought together and fertilised artificially, and then implanted in the womb. In this case the whole embryo has been donated – with no genetic link with either partner.

5. If either or both sperm and ovum are viable, but the woman cannot go through pregnancy and childbirth, it is possible to arrange surrogacy (womb leasing). Sperm and ovum are brought together – either being donated – and artificially implanted in the womb of the surrogate mother.

Some issues raised by this:

• The last three of these methods have been made possible by 'in-vitro fertilisation' (i.e. the natural process of fertilisation takes place in an artificial environment, literally 'in glass'). Is the development of this medical technique itself moral, immoral or amoral?

1. Most technical developments are amoral. For example, a fast car is not immoral in itself, but may become the occasion of immoral activity if it is driven in a way that endangers life. A first ethical point to decide is whether there should be limits to technology – a point at which the development and availability of a technology is in itself immoral. Here, of course, everything depends on the basis of your ethical argument –– whether natural law, utilitarianism, personal development, etc. A utilitarian argument (see Chapter 5) will justify a technology if it offers an increase in happiness; and on this basis, any medical technique is acceptable that people believe will improve their life. (Except, of course, if the cost of such operations means that other people are deprived of basic medical care.) If the criterion is personal development, then any technique which improves personal mental or physical performance is justified if wanted.

In setting your limits (if any) you might want to consider:

- Would you like (e.g. through genetic engineering) to be able to choose the sex and all the physical characteristics of your child? And, if so, would you like to live in a world where everyone's characteristics had been selected in this way?

- If it were possible, would you be prepared to authorise a brain transplant for someone close to you – enabling life to continue, but with a totally different set of mental characteristics and memories? Who would the 'new' person be?

- Would you authorise the development and use of a medical technique that could save lives, but would be so expensive that it would starve other medical services of funds? (This is a realistic and serious moral issue within any health service whose funds are limited.)

2. You might argue that, in a world where there are quite enough unwanted children, it is immoral to develop expensive techniques to conceive more. Infertile couples should be encouraged to adopt children instead.

3. You might argue, on the basis of natural law, that since the sexual act is the natural way in which fertilisation takes place, the attempt to replicate that process in a clinical environment detracts from the unique and personal context of natural fertilisation. If you take this line of argument, you may need to accept that many other medical techniques – from life-saving surgery to the use of antibiotics – could also be challenged. The whole basis of medicine is to change the natural course of disease or to make good a disability. A natural law basis for ethics could equally claim that this is the product of human reason, and that the development of medicine is therefore a natural human function, given the desire to relieve suffering.

• Where either semen or ovum (or both) has been provided by a donor, should the resulting child ever be given information about that donor or donors?

1. What is the basis of human individuality? Is it the genetic link with 'parents' (as providers of semen and ovum) or with 'parents' (as those who care for a child and bring it up)? Is the donor really a parent? You might want to contemplate the difference between a child who is adopted, and who claims the right to find out details of his or her natural parents, and the child who is actually born from the womb of his or her 'mother', but who finds that genetically he or she is linked with one (or two) unknown donors?

2. If the donor could be traced, should the child be able to inherit from that donor, or make any other claim? Alterna-

tively, should a donor be able to make any claim on a child born as a result of that donation?

- With surrogacy, this problem has an added complication, since the 'natural' mother and the 'parents' are in touch with one another, and the situation is reversed - in that it is the donor (or donors) who find themselves bringing up 'their' child.

1. In Britain, following the 1990 Human Fertilisation and Embryology Bill, the 'mother' in such cases is defined as the woman who gives birth, and the 'father' is her husband, provided that he has agreed to the procedure. (i.e. the person who donated the semen is not considered to be the legal father of the child, whether that person was an unknown donor or the person commissioning the surrogacy.) This means that the couple who want to use a surrogate mother place themselves in the position of donors – once the child is fertilised, the legal 'mother' is the person in whose womb that embryo is lodged. The commissioning couple then have to adopt the child once it is born – although this adoption cannot be made a legal requirement. It is possible for the surrogate mother to change her mind and refuse to hand over the child.

2. The surrogate mother may be a close relative of the donor couple, or previously unknown to them. She may give her services free, claim only her expenses, or (illegally in Britain) receive payment.

3. The British Medical Association (BMA) published a report on surrogacy in 1990, offering guidelines to doctors. The ethical basis recommended was that all decisions should be made in the best interests of the child. It advised that surrogacy should be considered only after the failure of all other methods of treatment.

- The conception of a child is a biological process, part of which may be carried out in an artificially constructed environment. But the birth is also a matter of personal relationships and the emotions associated with them. In a 'natural' context, these two features of human reproduction come together in an act of sex which leads to pregnancy and birth.

1. The BMA guidelines mentioned above take the basis of ethical decisions as the welfare of the child to be conceived – this is a utilitarian argument (see Chapter 5), based on expected results. A natural law argument would equally want to consider the welfare of the child that is to be born, but would do so in the context of whether or not the actual process of conceiving that child was in accordance with the understanding of the natural place of sex and childbirth in human life.

2. The issues involved with such medical procedures can be applied to a wide range of issues, e.g. genetic engineering, which involve the apparent overcoming of those situations when the natural process of life does not yield the results that people want.

3. A further ethical line to be considered here might be the right of the individuals concerned to have certain experiences in order to further their own personal development. We shall examine these arguments in Chapter 7, but you may wish to ask at this point: Is 'motherhood' or 'fatherhood' a right that people can claim on the grounds that they will not be fulfilled as a person unless they experience it?

4. In Britain, 90% of all treatments for infertility are done privately, and are quite expensive. Should infertility be treated as an illness, for which there should be free treatment?

• In an in-vitro fertilisation, several eggs may be fertilised successfully. If more than one is implanted successfully, the result is a multiple birth. There is, therefore, a limit to the number of fertilised embryos that can be used immediately. The remainder may be frozen – to be used later – discarded, or used for research.

1. The embryo has the potential to become a person – indeed, it already has the genetic information which will determine all the characteristics of that human being into which it will grow (given the right conditions). Should it therefore be treated as a person? Is it right to discard a 'person', or to use him or her for research?

2. In the normal course of events only about 60 per cent of embryos actually succeed in establishing themselves in the

womb and growing into babies, and in the case of in-vitro fertilisation the success rate is much lower. In depriving a 'spare' embryo of implantation, we are not depriving it of a certainty of development, but only of a possibility.

3. If the embryo does not become a human being at the point at which it is fertilised (and therefore genetically defined), at what point does this humanisation come about? This point is debated especially in the context of abortion, but it applies equally to all issues of fertility and the very early stages of life.

EUTHANASIA

Euthanasia is literally 'good death', and it is used in situations when death is deliberately chosen. Euthanasia is not concerned with situations where death happens by accident (a person with a painful illness might be killed in a motor accident), nor where death occurs as the secondary effect of, for example, failed medical treatment.

Euthanasia may be divided into four categories:

1. Suicide. This is self-administered euthanasia. Suicide is not illegal (although it may be considered morally wrong), but helping someone to commit suicide is illegal.

2. Voluntary euthanasia. This is carried out at the request of the person who wishes to die, but is not able to commit suicide, or for a person who is no longer able to ask to die, but has left prior instructions that he or she wishes to be helped to die in certain circumstances.

3. Involuntary euthanasia. This is when someone is killed in order to save him or her additional suffering, but when, in spite of being able to ask to die, the person has not actually done so. Like a child's visit to the dentist, it is imposed 'for his or her own good' but against his or her wishes.

4. Non-voluntary euthanasia. This is the killing of someone who is not in a position to ask to live or die (e.g. a person in a long-term coma following severe brain damage).

Possible action:

In practice, you can divide euthanasia into 'active' and 'passive'. Active euthanasia is where something is done actively to end life – e.g. the giving of a lethal injection. However good the motive, it is in some sense 'killing'. Passive euthanasia is 'allowing someone to die' by withholding treatment and letting nature take its course.

Examples:

Passive euthanasia – turning off a life support system to which a comatose patient has been connected.

Active euthanasia – in time of war, a mortally wounded soldier in great pain and distress, and may ask to be 'finished off' by a comrade in order to shorten his suffering.

- Under British law, a person has the right to refuse treatment, as long as he or she is fully competent to make that decision.

- If a patient is not in a position to ask for or refuse treatment (e.g. if unconscious) then a doctor can decide to withhold treatment. He or she is not required to consult with the patient's relatives about this, although it is considered good medical practice to do so.

- If a person dies as the result of treatment being stopped, relatives could be in a position to sue the doctor concerned. Because of this, a doctor can apply to a Court of Law to ask for a ruling on whether or not to discontinue treatment. The legal decision is a safeguard for the doctor.

- In Holland euthanasia is widely practised, although not strictly legal. Under guidelines drawn up by the Royal Dutch Medical Association, two doctors have to be involved, and, having helped someone to die, they inform the Dutch equivalent of the Director of Public Prosecutions that they have done so. It is accepted that no charges will be brought against them. In Holland, euthanasia accounts for about 8 per cent of deaths.

- In 1967 in the USA, a lawyer called Luis Kutner coined the term 'living will' for a document which sets out the conditions under which a person wishes to be allowed to die. Since then many millions of Americans have drawn up such a will, and most states have passed laws which protect the rights of someone who is dying to have his or her wishes followed. The suggested wording for this was:

> 'If I should have an incurable or irreversible condition that will cause my death within a relatively short time, and am no longer able to make decisions regarding my medical treatment, I direct my attending physician... to withhold or withdraw treatment that only prolongs the process of dying and is not necessary to my comfort or to alleviate pain.'
>
> (From an article by Ann Lloyd, *The Independent*, May 18th 1990)

SOME ETHICAL CONSIDERATIONS:

- Any justification of suicide and voluntary euthanasia is generally made on the grounds that death is preferable to the suffering that would be involved if the person continued to live – in other words it is based on expected results (relief from anticipated pain). This may be related to the pain, physical or emotional, that the individual suicide may be experiencing, or it may be the suffering of other people that the suicide seeks to avoid. For example, a person may sacrifice his or her life in order to give others a better chance of survival in a situation where the means of supporting life are limited. Equally, a person may be prepared to die in a suicide mission in order to support a political cause. In these cases, too, the basis in ethics is the expected results of the action.

- A traditional Catholic and 'natural law' approach would argue that suicide goes against the idea of humankind as the 'faithful steward' of a life given by God. In other words, by seeking death, one is avoiding the natural course of one's life, and the potential for making creative use of whatever happens, even if that involves suffering or personal distress. An exception to this might be the case of a religious person who is prepared to become a martyr rather than renounce his or her faith. In this case, the person concerned does not actually choose to die, but is determined to maintain his or her integrity. The death penalty is a secondary result, not the intended end of that act of defiance.

- The Oath of Hippocrates, originating from the 5th century BCE and taken (in one of a number of modern forms) by doctors, requires them to promise 'to give no deadly medicine to anyone if asked, nor suggest any such counsel.'

The problem here is that many medical treatments and drugs are 'deadly' if given in sufficient quantity, and there is a balance to be struck, especially in the case of those suffering from terminal illnesses, between giving sufficient drugs to keep them pain-free, and actually shortening their lives by doing so. In this case, the ethical principle used is called 'The Law of Double Effect' – you are only responsible for the intended result of your action, not for any secondary or unforeseen results. In this case, a doctor may feel justified in increasing the doses of a painkilling drug to the point at which the drug becomes lethal, simply because the alternative is to allow the patient to remain in intolerable pain. The intention is not to kill, simply to remove pain.

- In the case of non-voluntary euthanasia, you need to decide when a life begins and when it ends. Is a person who has been in a coma for a number of years actually alive? He or she may have natural functions – breathe, have a heartbeat and some residual brain activity – but is that really what we mean by human life?

- 'Pro-life' campaigns – although generally focused on the issue of abortion – are relevant here. If you argue that human life begins at the moment of conception, and ends at the moment of death, and that the person should be treated as a full human individual throughout the time between those two moments, then whether you are dealing with an unborn child or an unconscious adult, that individual should be protected in exactly the same way as a conscious adult. In this respect, abortion and euthanasia are often linked, and the ethical basis for this position is 'natural law', i.e. it is not that the unborn child is going to be happier by being born, not that the unconscious patient is going to experience benefit by being kept alive, simply that, by virtue of being a human individual, one should be allowed to fulfil whatever is one's natural life.

- Voluntary euthanasia societies generally argue that euthanasia should be allowed if:

  1. a person is diagnosed by two doctors as suffering from an incurable illness, likely to cause, pain, distress, etc.

  2. a person has made a written request for euthanasia if the situation in '1' should occur, at least thirty days beforehand.

  The moral basis for this position is respect for the human individual and the right of the individual to have his or her wishes followed.

- Euthanasia illustrates the ethical division between 'natural law' arguments and those based on 'situation ethics'. In the latter, a person should do whatever love requires in a particular situation —and that may allow euthanasia, both voluntary and non-voluntary.

- Underlying almost all of the points that have been made above is the basic question: Does human life have an intrinsic value, and, if so, how is that value defined? Quantity of life? Quality of life? Integrity of the individual? Contribution of the individual to society?

A SUMMARY

- For those who accept its philosophical and religious basis, 'natural law' gives a very straightforward and apparently objective way of deciding between right and wrong, avoiding many of the ambiguities of assessing expected results. It avoids the 'situation ethics' approach, where every individual situation has to be assessed, and offers general rules to be applied and adapted to fit particular dilemmas.

- We have also looked at the question of what it is to act in a 'natural' way and whether human reason should either follow or go against what is observed in the rest of nature.

- I hope to have illustrated here that, although reason – in formulating 'natural law' – is an important element in morality, it does not really cope with all the issues about what it is to be natural. Humankind may be a species that thinks, but it does much else besides, and not all its actions are framed by logical thought – there are other very powerful elements to be considered.

Whether or not an action can be justified by natural law, the examples given above have shown that many people consider the expected results of an action in order to decide if it is right or wrong, and it is to such utilitarian arguments that we now turn.

5

—LOOKING FOR— RESULTS

——— EGOISTIC HEDONISM ———

Egoism is the theory that, however we choose to behave, we actually do those things that we believe will benefit ourselves.

There are two ways of looking at egoism:

1. One could claim that – whether they accept it or not – people are in fact acting in their own best interests. A psychologist could argue, for example, that even those who appear to do things for the sake of others are in fact pleasing themselves in doing so. They may enjoy helping others, or they may delight in being thought of as kind and unselfish. Deep down they have a need to give themselves to others, a need to bolster their own sense of goodness by doing so, perhaps to cover some unacknowledged guilt. One could, therefore, be utterly unselfish for utterly selfish motives.

The jibe that the unselfish person is a 'do-gooder' may imply this form of egoism. If I say of someone that they are 'too good to be true' it may imply the same sense that, at some level, people naturally display selfish tendencies, and the total absence of them is suspicious.

On the other hand, we need to keep in mind that the aim of religion is often given as the breaking down of fundamental human selfishness. That people in their natural state are selfish, but that, through spiritual practices, they can genuinely overcome this. St Augustine (354-430) believed that all people had an evil impulse, as a direct result of the Fall of Adam, and that they could only be restrained by the coercive power of the state and the laws of the Church.

Hobbes (in *Leviathan*), argued that people are motivated by the desire for gain, for security and for their own glory. But others (e.g. Rousseau) have seen a natural state as one in which there is a desire to co-operate and feel pity towards others. In either case, this is in general a statement about what 'is' rather than about what 'ought to be' – and is therefore more a comment on the background or starting point for ethics, rather than a conclusion about how people should act.

Whether people are naturally selfish, and whether – through religion, therapy, rehabilitation programmes or the like – this selfishness can be overcome, is a matter for personal judgement. From an ethical point of view, the second view of egoism is more important:

2. An ethical egoist is someone who claims that everybody should in fact pursue his or her own best interest. Here, selfishness is a policy, not a fact to be regretted. Few thinkers have argued this is a very stark fashion. Perhaps the most obvious is Machiavelli (1469-1527), whom we shall consider again in the next chapter. He certainly claimed that people will do what is right only under compulsion, and that generally, given the chance, they will do what they want for themselves. Ambition, and the desire to gain power, are what really motivate people. But Machiavelli was not strictly an ethical egoist, for he did not say that one could *define* what was right or wrong by reference to self-interest, only that, in the practical business of politics, in order to maintain the integrity and success of the state, a prince must be prepared to do what appears to be evil. He says, for example, that one should not keep promises if that goes against your own self-interest, or if the reason for making the promise in the first place has now changed.

According to an egoist ethic, the one obligation on an individual is to do that which benefits himself or herself. There is no moral responsibility to help others; you do so only if it pleases you to do so – and therefore that you do it for your own benefit.

On this basis, personal success in life is the basic motivation for all action, and the justification for what is done. We shall see later (Chapter 7) that personal development is one of the platforms from which we can view the range of values and decisions open to us – but ethical egoism makes it the *only* one.

An example:

If you are a genuine egoist and recommend that attitude to others, they are likely to develop themselves in a way that threatens you. Egoism is a benefit to you as long as others do not adopt it.

> *A manager, interviewing two candidates for the post of his immediate subordinate, recognises that one of them will do the job adequately, and the other is likely to be brilliant at it. Which should he appoint?*

If he is an egoist, the manager will certainly appoint the less able candidate, on the grounds that the brilliant one will progress to the point that he will take over the manager's own job. The task of an egoist is to restrain the development of those whose rise will threaten him, and utilise the powers of those who will not.

Hedonism is the term used to describe an attitude which makes happiness the goal of life.

Epicurus founded the school of philosophy in Athens in 307/6 BCE which was named after him. He held that judgements we make are based on our feeling of pleasure or pain. But this is not simple sensuality – for Epicureans held that intellectual enjoyment was pleasure worth seeking. Nor did the Epicureans indulge themselves, but lived quite simply. They held that mental pleasure was better than physical, and that fulfilments of the mind were superior to pleasures of the body. The main thing was to have peace of mind.

So hedonism is not always a matter of crude or immediate

enjoyment. An athlete may taking up training to run a race, and may suffer in doing it, but overall the experience of the training and the race may be positive – something worthwhile, in spite of the work involved.

To act only in your own interest – to get maximum satisfaction – is the main feature of egoistic hedonism. Jeremy Bentham (1748 -1832) may be seen as one of the chief exponents of egoistic hedonism. He thought that people generally act in such a way as to maximise their own pleasure. Yet he himself was a philanthropist – but one who explained that he found pleasure in helping others.

Perhaps, with the help of a psychoanalyst, one could come to the conclusion that almost all human responses, however altruistic, were ultimately based on selfishness. You cannot argue against the claim of unconscious motivation - I may not think that I am being selfish in making a credit card donation after watching a television appeal, but am I? What am I really seeking to gain? A sense of having done something worthwhile? Less guilt at seeing people starve on the television while eating my supper in front of the screen? A sense of satisfaction and identity with similarly charitably disposed people?

It's hard to be a radically honest egoistic hedonist. You are not free to be unselfish. You also have the conviction that every helpful person who is apparently trying to do something for you is in fact doing something for himself or herself instead – you are simply being made the occasion of that person's happiness.

An example

> *'I'll carry it myself and hope you feel guilty!'*

I shall feel pleased to have denied you the opportunity of helping. I am acting in my own best interest, and an aching back is a small price to pay for having cheated a do-gooder out of doing good!

Having said that, one of the main sources of happiness is the sense that life has a purpose, and that you are fulfilling yourself within it. That, in all probability will involve other people and your relationship with them, therefore ethics – which determines the satisfactory relationship with others, is also about a major source of happiness.

But happiness is not always proportional to what might be seen as goodness – you have to consider the long-term happiness. So, for example, if I come across a vulnerable old person in a dark alley with a bulging handbag, spilling over with banknotes, the prospect of a quick snatch might, in the short term, give me considerable pleasure. In the long term, it has to be weighed against the likelihood of being caught and punished for the action, or my own conscience at having gained by causing another person to suffer. Or even, if I live to be old, the fear of walking down dark alleys while carrying all the wealth I have accumulated by such actions in the past.

You could argue, therefore, that there is short term selfishness: I want that now! and long term selfishness: I will enjoy life more if I follow these principles etc. But in this case, selfishness may actually be something that benefits others. In this case 'selfishness' does not refer so much to the expected outcome, but to the motivation. Thus a person may be selfish by intention, but actually end up with unhappiness – since what is sought may bring only illusory happiness.

Examples:

That extra drink before you drive may taste good, and may supply the happiness and sense of global harmony and universal insight which comes with mild intoxication. In the longer term, it may be a very short lived happiness that is soon to be regretted.

The sexual urge may be hard to resist – it promises an intense happiness of regrettably short duration. That condomless moment of passion needs to be weighed against the result of HIV infection. Refusing to have unprotected sex is not a rejection of happiness, but a deferment of happiness – preferring the security of health (with the prospect of future sexual encounters) rather than an immediate risk.

If our duty is to pursue our own greatest pleasure (which is basic to the hedonistic position), then what follows is largely decided by how we define pleasure, and whether we take a short or long view.

- Do you only refrain from doing something for fear of being caught and punished? (That would be a radically hedonistic position.)

There is a sense in which egoistic hedonism is often self-defeating: as in the old joke, where a masochist encounters a sadist. Thinking that this could be the start of a really useful relationship, the masochist cries 'Hurt me!', but the sadist (being a sadist) replies 'No!' – an example of deferred pleasure!

Both Plato and Aristotle held the view that it is in a person's own best interest to act rightly. In this case, pleasure comes from doing good. But this is rather different from saying that pleasure is the same thing as goodness. They both argued for an objective idea of goodness, and then showed that following it would be beneficial.

However much it may be used to illustrate the way in which people sometimes act, egoistic hedonism is very difficult to sustain as an ethic to be shared with others, to account for the experience of moral choice, conscience and the like.

Nevertheless, in making a moral choice, it is natural that a person should hope that happiness, or benefit of some sort, should come from making the right decision. In other words, consequences or results cannot be ignored – but the assessment of them generally takes other people (or the situation as a whole) into account, and not just the benefit of the person taking the choice. This therefore leads naturally into the ethical theory called *utilitarianism*.

—————— UTILITARIANISM ——————

Bentham argued for the 'Principle of Utility', by which he meant that an action should be judged according to the results it achieved. This approach to ethics is called *utilitarianism*, and it has been one of the most influential of ethical theories – and the one most widely used in ordinary 'common-sense' decisions.

In contrast to Bentham, whose view is basically hedonistic, the person who developed utilitarianism into the form most commonly recognised today was John Stuart Mill (1806-1873). He argued (in *Utilitarianism* 1861) that the happiness should not be simply one's own, but that of the greatest number. In adding this, he gives the possibility of some higher sense of moral obligation; we act out of a general desire to do what is right for the benefit of all, not simply for our own happiness, within whatever constraints are imposed upon us.

In its simplest form, utilitarianism states that in any situation where there is a moral choice to make, the right thing to do is that which is likely to produce the greatest happiness for the greatest number of people.

Now, this seems a very straightforward approach to ethical decisions. But it raises two important points:

1. How do you evaluate the results of an action?

- Is 'happiness' to be judged by a person's feelings alone, or is there some more objective way of assessing it?

- What are your criteria for saying that a result is 'good'?

- Should you consider only the immediate happiness that an action brings, or should you rather look to its long-term consequences?

For example, a doctor, administering first-aid at the scene of an accident, may need to cause additional pain by straightening a broken limb. Is that pain good or bad?

Clearly, the benefit of having a limb that is set straight is worth the short-term pain involved. On the other hand, suppose that the person with the perfectly restored leg is now able to run. He sees a taxi and makes a dash across the road in order to get it. Although he is quick, he is not quick enough, and is killed by a passing car. The end result of having a leg capable of running is that the person is dead. With a limp, he would have remained on the side of the road in otherwise good health.

Now, if the fact of the person's subsequent accident were known at the time, it might be judged prudent to leave the person with a limp. The implication of this is that every time one makes a decision, one tries to take into account all the possible results of that action. But those results will be constantly changing, since everything that happens continues to have repercussions that are not known at the time. In which case, there can never be a moment at which it is possible to say that the amount of happiness caused will definitely outweigh the amount of harm.

Let us make this situation absolutely clear by taking the most blunt of hypothetical examples:

Imagine you are in a position to save the life of a young boy in mortal danger. You might rightly assume that it is better for him to be alive than dead. The act of saving him is therefore morally right. But suppose the boy happens to be called Adolf Hitler? With hindsight you might then feel that the result of saving that life was to cause far more suffering than allowing him to die.

Here then is the dilemma of a simple utilitarian approach. You are never in a position to know with absolute certainty the relative amounts of happiness or pain that any action will cause.

2. The actual results of an action may also be ambiguous.

* How do you balance the unhappiness caused to one person against the happiness of many?

* Is immediate happiness the criterion, or is it the longer term benefit?

For example, some would recommend that young offenders should be given a prison sentence, in the hope that it would encourage them to reform and thus not re-offend. This could imply that, although not experienced as such, the punishment is regarded as increasing the happiness of the offender in the long term, as well as offering added happiness to those in society that he or she will not be able to offend against.

* By what criteria do you judge what leads to happiness in this case? If you act against someone's wishes, claiming that it is 'really' for their greater happiness, you presumably do so on the basis of your idea of what constitutes the good life. On what is that idea based?

The smiling headmaster of old who brandished a cane saying 'it's for your own good!' may have believed just that. But could it be proved? More and more evidence could be brought, and yet there would never be certainty. Some would point to occasions of genuine reform, others to establishing a cult of brutality.

The assumption here is twofold:

1. That a person is reformed through punishment, and will, as a result of that reformation, enjoy greater happiness in the future.

2. That society as a whole will experience greater happiness through freedom from the threat of the unreformed person.

There is a further dilemma as we try to balance the harm that may be inflicted on one person against the resulting happiness of a greater number. Here we come against the dilemma of hostages or the use of warfare to settle disputes:

An example

The Falklands War

Great Britain went to war with Argentina over the invasion by the latter of the Falkland Islands in the South Atlantic. The war was costly, both in terms of the men killed on both sides, and in terms of the weapons and ships destroyed, and the resulting cost of maintaining troops on the islands. As a result of it the Argentine invasion was repelled, and the islands returned to British rule.

From a straightforward utilitarian position one might argue that it would be better to allow the Falklands to be taken over, rather than suffer such loss of life.

On the other hand, Margaret Thatcher, the British Prime Minister at the time, made clear that the decision to go to war was based on the absolute right to defend British sovereignty. This was a principle itself worth defending, apparently regardless of the cost involved.

Yet, underlying this principle, there was another argument used, this time a utilitarian one – namely that if once Britain decided that, because of the small numbers of islanders affected, it was not worth defending the Falklands, then all other small dependencies would feel insecure, knowing that, if threatened, Britain would not come to their aid. Here we have a clearly utilitarian backing for a principle.

Notice that what we have here is a utilitarian backing for the imposition of a general principle – not a utilitarian assessment of a particular situation in isolation. This is important, because it points towards a variation of the utilitarian argument – 'rule utilitarianism' to which we shall turn in a moment.

- THREE FORMS OF UTILITARIANISM -

ACT UTILITARIANISM

This is the form of the argument that we have been considering to date. It looks for the results of an individual act in order to assess whether the act is right or wrong. In this form, utilitarianism accepts no general rules, except the rule that one should seek the greatest happiness of the greatest number.

This form of the argument offers no way of deciding between two conflicting views as to what constitutes the greatest pleasure. It also comes up against many of the problems of assessing results that we have outlined and illustrated above.

One final point about act utilitarianism is that it requires an assessment about pain or happiness which is related to each individual action. But the perceived results of an action may be only explicable in terms of social convention, not in terms of actual pain inflicted. People may choose to suffer – for them it is their happiness – but this may not be perceived by the external observer.

An example

You observe a scene of extreme suffering. A crowd of people hobbling, shuffling and obviously in pain, run between lines of onlookers. You observe their exhaustion, and learn that they have run 26 miles, and, in doing so, they have suffered blisters, cramp and other aches and pains. Suppose you see one of them, at the limit of his or her endurance, slow to a walking pace, but the crowd of onlookers shout that he or she should continue running. Such action would be regarded as cruelty of a mass scale.

Yet thousands of people the world over will choose to go through just such an ordeal, pushing themselves to the limit. Voluntary suffering may be idiotic, but it is not immoral, unless, by accepting it, genuine harm is done to others. If a person is determined to run a marathon in spite of medical warnings to the contrary, risks his or her life, and thereby risks all the suffering that their death could cause their family, that might be regarded as immoral. Otherwise, running a marathon is an example of the acceptance of pain for no obvious result (other than that of personal satisfaction).

Pleasure and pain are therefore to be set in a social context, and may be misunderstood. It might be possible – for example, by arguing that it inspires others to get fit – to justify a marathon in strictly utilitarian terms, but it is by no means the straightforward assessment of pain or pleasure that act utilitarianism assumes.

RULE UTILITARIANISM

This rather more sophisticated approach to utilitarianism was put forward by John Stuart Mill. He argued:

- That intellectual pleasures should be preferred to immediate physical pleasures, and that the quality of the pleasure anticipated as well as the quantity. (In this he followed the Epicurean tradition.)

- That justice required that each person should count as an individual, irrespective of the intensity of pleasure or pain involved.

But he took an important step in allowing respect for those rules that were formed for the benefit of the whole of society. The rule not to kill, for example, is framed for the benefit of society as a whole. Thus the utilitarian can use general rules and principles, on the grounds that those principles have themselves been framed on utilitarian grounds.

This is the basis (given in the example of the Falklands War, above) for saying that one should uphold the right of national sovereignty – since the security offered by that rule is to the benefit of humanity as a whole.

As it has developed, those who take this line of argument have divided between:

- **strong rule utilitarians**, who hold that one should not break one of these general rules to fit individual situations

- **weak rule utilitarians**, who would allow the particular pleasure or pain involved in a particular situation to take precedence over the general rule, whilst still allowing the general rule and its benefits to be taken into consideration.

PREFERENCE UTILITARIANISM

This form of the argument says that you should take into account the preferences of the person concerned in each case – unless those preferences are outweighed by the preferences of others.

In other words, this form allows the people concerned to say what for them constitutes pleasure or pain. It does not allow the person acting to impose his or her own criterion of pleasure on other people.

Notice that Utilitarianism works in a way that is the opposite to that of Natural Law. Natural Law starts with theories about the nature of the world and the purpose in life. From those general theories, it looks at each and every action and object and asks about its purpose. Once that is known, it claims that the right thing to do it that which fulfils the natural purpose, and the wrong thing is that which frustrates it. You start from principles, and apply them to individual situations.

When we come to Utilitarianism, the opposite is the case. We start with the pain or pleasure involved in individual situations, and then take into account the wider pain or pleasure involved by the application of general rules, or the preferences of the people involved. The starting point, however, is with the immediate situation.

What the two approaches have in common is their desire to find some external, objective criterion (whether the pleasure or pain involved, or the purpose to be fulfilled) by which to show that an action is right or wrong.

In theory, using either of these approaches, it should be possible to present a case for morality which is convincing to other people, for it can be set out and demonstrated.

The limitation of this approach, as we have seen, is that there is never enough evidence to provide certainty. Everything is open to the possibility of future results which will outweigh the present assessment.

── SEX AND UTILITARIANISM ──

In the chapter on 'natural law' we saw that, for those following that type of argument, the natural function of sex was the conception of children, and that this was its justification. Sex that deliberately sought to frustrate this (e.g. through contraception), or which did not have it as a possible outcome (e.g. homosexuality or masturbation), was therefore wrong.

In practice, however, for what appears to be a majority of people, sexual morality is assessed on a utilitarian basis. It might be considered right to have sexual intercourse provided:

- that if it takes place in private (nobody else is involved or likely to be offended by it)

- that if the partners consent to it (it is considered by them to increase their own happiness)

- that it does not harm others.

'It's not hurting anyone. We want to. So why shouldn't we?'

This statement about sexual morality is utilitarian. Now try to imagine how a parent might respond if this is the attitude of his or her son or daughter. Here are three lines of approach:

1. *'It's wrong, unless you're married.'*

or 2. *'It will lead to unhappiness because.... '*

or 3. *'If you're going to have sex anyway, at least make sure you use contraception.'*

- In the first case, there is an absolute rule. This could be backed up by natural law, but if challenged, many would give a string of reasons why sex outside marriage is not a good idea, and most of these would be based on results.

- The basis of the second response is clearly utilitarian and may become the 'fall back' position of someone who starts with the first response and is then challenged.

- The third response is also utilitarian, taking a positive approach to minimise possible harmful effects, and thus tip the balance of happiness in favour of having sex rather than not.

Although the actual position between young person and parent may sound very different – the one libertarian and the other authoritarian – they may well actually be using the same utilitarian methods of assessing the situation.

Notice that, for example, in advertising about contraception and the risks of HIV infection, the moral arguments in favour of taking a 'responsible' attitude to sex are utilitarian. Indeed, the major shift in sexual attitudes brought about by the threat of HIV and AIDS, is largely due to the threat of harmful results, and these, when taken seriously, become the basis of 'responsible' behaviour on a utilitarian view.

The same sort of utilitarian argument surrounds issues of adultery and the break up of marriages. Very often debate focuses not on the actual sexual desire of one person for someone who is not their marriage partner, nor on the morality of their sexual relationship as such, but on the potential harm that this might to do others – especially children of the marriage.

Sexual attraction outside marriage may be presented as the cause of so many single-parent families, which in turn may be the reason why so many people are dependent on state help. The sexual act is therefore not condemned from a traditional 'rule based' standpoint, but from one which highlights the social and economic consequences.

I am not arguing here that the utilitarian view is necessarily the right one with regard to sexual morality, but that it is implied by much current debate on sexual issues.

- SOME ISSUES IN MEDICAL ETHICS -

Medical ethics is concerned with the moral principles by which doctors and other therapists decide how they should treat patients, and with the way in which medical technology as a whole should be used within society.

Medical ethics is seldom based on utilitarian principles alone – for there are serious questions about the meaning of 'health' and general principles about the value of human life to be taken into consideration. There are also questions about when life starts and when it ends. Medicine may be practised by those who see it as an expression of their own religious commitment, and expressing their particularly religious values.

Nevertheless, some of the most topical medical questions are considered in a way that reflects a utilitarian approach to ethics.

RESEARCH

In 1964, the World Medical Association set out principles which were intended to guide doctors who were to be involved with medical research. Two of these principles are definitely utilitarian. They are:

- That the objectives of the research should be in proportion to the inherent risk to the subject. (In other words, the likely results should justify what is being done.)

- Before starting any clinical trial, the risks involved should be assessed in terms of the foreseeable benefits to the subject. (In other words, the person taking part in the medical trial should be expected to benefit personally. It would not be acceptable to expect a person to accept a risk just for the sake of some future unspecified gain in medical knowledge, however important that might be held to be.)

An example

> *During the Second World War, medical experiments were forcibly carried out on inmates of concentration camps.*

These were regarded as crimes, because there was no intention to offer the subjects any benefit from them – they were harmed simply for the sake of gaining medical knowledge.

ORGAN TRANSPLANTS

There are two ways in which utilitarian arguments are used in this issue. Let us consider the situation with kidney transplants. Many thousands of people suffer kidney transplants in Britain each year. There are not sufficient medical facilities to treat them all. Some die as a result. There are a significant number at any one time waiting for a kidney transplant. **If** doctors were allowed to take the kidneys from any healthy person who was killed in an accident, more patients would benefit. This might suggest that there should be an 'opt out' clause for the transplantation of organs, so that doctors could be free to operate on anyone who had died unless he or she carried some identification deliberately forbidding such an operation. (At the moment, permission has to be obtained from next of kin, often in very difficult circumstances.)

A situation:

'Organs may be preserved without permission'

'A scheme to preserve the organs of accident victims without the permission of relatives could soon be adopted across the country, a leading transplant surgeon said.

'Under an earlier initiative, doctors at Leicester University suffused the kidneys of nine corpses with ice-cold fluid while they sought approval to remove the organs. In eight cases, the relatives agreed.

'Under the proposal, bodies would be kept cool by chilled preservation fluid, pumped into the kidneys through a catheter. The donors would be both 'biblically dead' (their hearts would have stopped) as well as brain dead....

'The move is the latest step towards tackling record transplant waiting lists after doctors came under fire for removing organs from brain-dead donors whose hearts were kept beating.

'At the moment [in Britain] there are 4,300 people waiting for kidneys, 300 for hearts, 200 for heart-lungs and 100 for livers. Surgeons claim that every kidney transplant saves £40,000 over five years because of the high cost of dialysis.'

[From an article by Peter Pallot, *The Daily Telegraph*, June 21st 1993]

Issues here are:

- freedom of the individual (to allow or forbid transplantation of organs)

- whether or not a dead person has rights

- whether a relative of a recently deceased person is morally justified in refusing leave to transplant organs, given the benefit that can be gained by doing so

- whether the scale of human medical need should be allowed to overrule other considerations – allowing automatic removal of suitable organs, including those of brain-dead but artificially sustained patients.

A second moral issue regarding transplantation is quite different. It examines the cost of transplant operations, and compares it with the benefit to the health of people through routine screening and other less costly forms of treatment. A utilitarian might then ask if it is right to give one person a heart transplant, if the money for that operation could in fact have been used to benefit a greater number of people with less dramatic illnesses. This is not the same as the comparison given above between the cost of surgery and that of maintaining a person on dialysis, but whether the cost of either is justified, given the state of human health globally, following a strictly utilitarian moral line.

Sometimes, transplantation involves a living donor. This is the case with bone-marrow transplants, and the donor is often a close relative (because of the problem of compatibility). In the case of a relative, or a volunteer that is discovered as a result of the search for a compatible donor, there is little by way of a moral problem. A person is free to give something for the benefit of another. On the other hand, should you create a person in order for them to become a donor? This rare moral dilemma is a real one.

An example:

It was reported in the press in April 1990 that a woman in the United States had decided to have a second child, in order that the baby might provide bone marrow suitable for transplanting into her 17-year-old daughter, who suffered from leukaemia.

This step was taken because a nationwide search had failed to find any compatible donors. Tests on the mother showed that the then unborn child was a girl, and that she had a 99 per cent chance of being a compatible donor.

- Is it right to bring a child into the world with the specific intention of using that life to save another, even that of a close relative?

A strictly utilitarian argument would say that it is, provided that the newly born child did not risk death as a result of giving life. Those whose ethics are closer to the 'natural law' approach might argue that it is a misuse of the process of giving birth to do so only for the secondary reason of saving someone else. On the other hand, you might want to argue that many children are conceived as a

---

result of a failure of contraception - is that more moral than to conceive for a specific purpose? What of the person who conceives a child in order to have an heir to inherit a personal fortune? Is that any more or less manipulative than to conceive in order to use the child for a more immediate life-saving medical process?

[reported in *The Independent* April 4th 1990]

There are general questions to be asked about the morally acceptable limits of medical and scientific procedures. Are such procedures to be evaluated in terms of potential benefits to be gained in the future? If so, it is very difficult to specify exactly how much is to be gained, or from what particular experiments. One of the main areas here is the use of 'spare' embryos – collections of cells that could, in suitable circumstances, develop into a human being – for experimentation. The argument against such experimentation is based largely on when human life is considered to begin – and therefore whether the use of these early embryos is the killing of human beings. The argument in favour is one based on a utilitarian assessment of the potential benefit to be gained from such experimental work.

In many of these debates, we see that two different forms of ethical argument are set against one another – 'natural law' (or at least a general view of the nature and rights of a human being) is set against 'utilitarianism', representing the results that are anticipated.

The utilitarian basis for moral decisions is clearly presented by the following comments from a person who has the task of managing the resources within the British Health Service:

A *situation:*

A consultant physician to an intensive care unit in London, commenting in March 1993 about financial priorities and the cost of intensive care units, said:

'Hospital managements may face the stark choice of spending £100,000 to keep a hopelessly damaged individual in intensive care for two months or allow him to die and perhaps spending the

money on four kidney transplants.'
Terminally ill patients occupying beds in intensive care might lessen the chance of heart patients having a life-saving operation in time or the essential access to post-operative skills.
The problem can only worsen given an ageing population that expects the very latest in medical science to be available to all.
[From an article by Christine Doyle, *The Daily Telegraph*,
March 16th 1993]

GENERAL CRITICISMS OF UTILITARIANISM

- Society is complex. It does not consist of uniform people, all wanting the same things, or expressing the same preferences. There will always be conflict of interests, divergences of views. Now utilitarianism has taken this into account to a certain extent by allowing for 'preferences' to be expressed, rather than imposing on others what we consider to be best for their greatest happiness. Nevertheless, the final decision is made in the interests of the majority. As we have seen in the section on medical ethics above, this means that it is very difficult to justify action on behalf of an individual or minority group. Any sense of social justice seems to demand that there should be cases where the majority freely gives up something to their benefit for the sake of a minority or an individual.

Example:

Sometimes, as a result of an appeal on television, the attention of a whole nation is focused on the plight of an individual. This is made especially poignant if the individual is a child desperate for a life-saving operation, or some local hero who is injured in the course of helping others. In these circumstances, offers of help are given which are out of all proportion to what would be allocated on a strictly utilitarian assessment of need.

- Are these the result of emotional indulgence rather than rational assessment of need?

- If so, is it wrong to have given help to an individual in these circumstances?

A utilitarian assessment may preclude action being taken on behalf of an individual, on the grounds that it is not in the interests of the majority that so much relief should be expended on a single person. On the other hand, if the majority are presented with the facts in a way that engages them emotionally, they may well freely give up something (generally money, offered to the needy cause) in order that the individual may benefit. In this case ' giving the greatest happiness to the greatest number of people' involves helping the individual, since the many who give also find happiness in doing so.

This would imply that a utilitarian argument may mistake what people actually want for what it is assumed that they should want. Charitable responses are often surprising.

- Utilitarianism deflects our attention from the personal convictions and values that lie at the heart of moral choices, and instead make the decision open to external assessment and calculation. As far as moral agency goes, it turns the creative artist into a bureaucrat! Moral responses are not always a matter of conforming to what is reasonable, but of acting out of convictions which may well require choices which may not obviously seem to bring happiness, but which are nevertheless felt to be 'right'.

I cannot always wait to think of the overall balance of happiness. My response, often spontaneous, is based on convictions, not calculations.

Examples:

A father, walking along a river bank, hears a shout from behind him and sees his child topple off a bicycle into the raging torrent. He plunges into the water, but is swept to his death, along with his child.

- A utilitarian, confronted with information about his remaining five, now fatherless, children, and his work as a surgeon, saving the lives of many, might say that he should not, on balance, have plunged into the water.

- But is it possible, in all honesty, to say that he was not acting morally in attempting that hopeless rescue? And who, listening to the oration at such a person's funeral would not wish, if put to a similar test, to have similar courage?

- I am not arguing that a person who did not attempt the rescue could not perfectly well have justified his or her decision to stand by and watch the child drown. Indeed, it might take great courage to do that. But is it the only morally correct option?

Perhaps a situation which illustrates this in its starkest form is given in William Styron's novel Sophie's Choice. *It explores the guilt of a woman living in the United States, who had survived a Nazi concentration camp. Gradually the source of her terrible sense of guilt is revealed. She was held in the camp with her two children. She was then given the choice, she could choose to save one of them, with the other sent to die. But she must choose which. If not, both will die. She makes the choice, knowing that, by doing so, she has condemned the other. She is haunted by that choice.*

- From a utilitarian point of view, she did the right thing. To have refused to have made a choice would have made it certain that both children would die.

- Equally, she is not to blame, since she did not actually choose that either child should die – she was not directly the agent of their deaths.

- But is it possible to live with such a choice? Does a utilitarian justification actually make the decision any more bearable?

There would seem to be two major limitations to the utilitarian standpoint:

1. Utilitarianism, because it focuses on results, which are external to the person making the moral choice, and able to be set out in an objective way, does not adequately take into account the motive for making a choice – and yet it is motivation which would seem to be important in the assessment of whether a person was behaving in a moral way.

2. Utilitarianism does not explain why it is that people sometimes feel that there are moral rules that should not be broken, irrespective of the consequences. This is a feature of moral dilemmas, and it is one to which we shall turn in the next chapter.

6

THE EXPERIENCE OF MORAL CHOICE

In the previous chapters we have examined two ways in which it is possible to justify moral claims – the first with reference to 'natural law', and the second based on the expected results. Both of these seek an external, objective basis for moral claims, examined rationally.

But there can be quite a different approach: to start not with reason but with experience. What does it mean for us to experience a sense of right and wrong, to have a conscience, or a conviction that one particular line of action is the right thing to do, quite apart from any expected consequences it may have?

The philosopher David Hume (in his *A Treatise on Human Nature* 1738) pointed out that, when all the relevant facts were known, there would still be no way of proving what 'ought' or 'ought not' to be done. Facts show what 'is', not what 'ought to be' – in other words, morality is to be based on a person's feelings. Just as we might call something beautiful, without there being any one particular thing that **proves** it to be beautiful – so we may call something right or wrong, based on the same subjective approval or disapproval. He also recognised that moral statements were a commitment to action, rather than just an observation. To say something is right is equivalent to saying that, in these particular circumstances, this is the thing to do.

But he points out that most writers are not careful to make this distinction:

'In every system of morality, which I have hitherto met with, I have always remarked, that the author proceeds for some time in the ordinary way of reasoning, and establishes the being of a God, or makes observations concerning human affairs; when of a sudden I am surprised to find, that instead of the usual copulations of propositions, *is* and *is not*, I meet with no proposition that is not connected with an *ought,* or an *ought not*. This change is imperceptible; but is, however, of the last consequence. For as this *ought*, or *ought not*, expresses some new relation or affirmation, it is necessary that it should be observed and explained; and at the same time that a reason should be given, for what seems altogether inconceivable, how this new relation can be a deduction from others, which are entirely different from it. But as authors do not commonly use this precaution, I shall presume to recommend it to the readers; and am persuaded, that this small attention would subvert all the vulgar systems of morality, and let us see, that the distinction of vice and virtue is not founded merely on the relations of objects, nor is perceived by reason.'

Hume, D, *A Treatise on Human Nature*, 1738

You may recognise in Hume a forerunner of some of the modern arguments about the meaning of moral statements that were examined in Chapter 3. What it is important to notice about Hume is that he pointed out clearly that moral statements were not a matter of observation, but of emotion and commitment. In other words, making a moral statement is a positive activity, in which the person making it has a creative part to play. Morality is not just about what exists 'out there', but how you see it, evaluate it, and respond to it.

— THE CATEGORICAL IMPERATIVE —

We therefore need to shift our examination of morality away from results towards the experience of a moral demand – the sense that I 'ought' to do something regardless of consequences. This is sometimes called the 'categorical imperative'.

- A 'hypothetical imperative' takes the form – 'If you want to achieve X then do Y.'

- A 'categorical imperative' takes the form – 'You should do Y.' It is absolute, having no conditions attached to it.

In this chapter we shall be looking at the categorical imperative, what it implies, and if it is a universal experience or necessary for morality.

The thinker most associated with this 'categorical imperative' is Immanuel Kant (1724-1804). Being an 18th century German Protestant, he was very much concerned with the sense of duty. You do your duty - what you understand to be right – without regard to consequences. His main work on this is *Fundamental Principles of the Metaphysics of Morals* (1785).

Kant held that the categories we use to understand the world – categories like space, time and causality – are not to be found in the data of our experience, but are imposed on our experience by our own minds. We cannot prove that everything has a cause – but our minds automatically look for causes. The mind plays an active part in shaping and ordering experience, it is not merely a passive recipient of what is 'out there'. This is sometimes referred to as Kant's 'Copernican Revolution' – just as Copernicus showed that the Earth revolved round the Sun, and not vice versa, so Kant showed that our minds determine the way in which we experience things.

In the same way, Kant argued that we would never be able to show conclusively that a certain action was right or wrong by reference to its expected results, because we would never have enough evidence, and might disagree about how to interpret it. The starting point for morals cannot therefore be something 'out there' among the data interpreted by our senses, but the actual experience of moral obligation – the feeling that there is something we 'ought' to do.

In other words, you do not first find out what is 'right' and then decide that you ought to do it; rather, that which you feel you ought to do is what you mean by 'right'.

Kant argued that to do your duty you have to exclude two other considerations – effects (or results) and inclinations. If you decide to do something, expecting that you will benefit by it – that is not a moral choice. Equally, if you decide to do something because you enjoy doing it, that is not a moral choice either. Kant also rejected external moral authority, where it conflicted with personal moral conviction. Unthinking obedience is not a valid moral position – one should act out of a personal sense of what is right.

Kant developed an abstract concept of morality – a principle which he thought would apply (in theory) to all situations. There are several different forms of this categorical imperative, but they include two main themes:

- Act only on that maxim (or principle) which you can – at the same time – will that it should become a universal law.

- Act in such a way as to treat people as ends and never as means.

The implication of the first, and major theme is that I should only do something if I am prepared for everyone else to be able to do it as well.

Notice what this does *not* tell you. It does not tell you what the content of your moral decision should be; it does not say that this or that action is always right or wrong. Rather it provides a general principle – that of our willingness to see the basis of our action become a universal law.

Examples:

Suicide

What if everyone chose to commit suicide? That would be the end of the human species, and therefore, following Kant's theory that something is only moral if I could wish it to become a universal law, it would seem to be wrong.

But is that necessarily the case?

- If I am suffering from a serious and incurable illness, I

---

might wish that everyone, should they ever be in this same situation, should be morally justified in choosing to end their life? It might be quite possible to hold the view that no healthy person should commit suicide, but that someone in terminal pain should be allowed to do so. So it is not clear that - following Kant's theory – one should rule out suicide entirely.

- Perhaps an important distinction is between what is compulsory and what is voluntary. If compulsory euthanasia on a universal scale is unacceptable, then it is morally wrong in each particular case. But to say that everyone should be free to choose this option is not to make it a universal law – just a universal option, which is a very different thing.

Telling the truth

Is it ever morally right to tell a lie? One has to ask about the possibility of willing, at the moment in which I am about to tell a lie, that it should be permitted for everyone else to tell lies as well. If I would not want to universalise the principle, then I would be morally wrong in telling lies in this particular situation.

There is a general question to ask of a theory such as Kant's: Is it possible to give a general rule which can be applied to a particular act, or is it essential to know the particular purpose and context of that act, and then decide on its merits in the light of them?

In the case of suicide, no two people are exactly the same, and nobody can know exactly the scale and quality of another person's suffering. Is it realistic to offer a general guideline of suicide? Should a person who chooses to take his or her own life be able to say 'I would wish that everyone suffering as I am at this moment, to be allowed to end his or her life.' If so, then on Kant's criterion of universalisability, that should be a morally correct thing to do.

A *situation*:

You are held by a terrorist gang, who demand to know the whereabouts of a close friend or relative whom they clearly wish to kill. You know that the person concerned is in hiding. Do you tell the truth and admit that you know where they are, or do you tell a lie, either by giving the wrong location, or by saying that you do not know where they are?

- Here there needs to be a balance between the expected results, and the application of a universal law.

- You might want to argue that anyone, confronted similarly by the prospect of the death of an innocent person, should lie. In this case, although the rule about telling the truth could be universalised, so also could the rule about doing anything necessary in order to prevent innocent suffering.

Kant accepts such a situation. The example he gives (*op cit* section II para 36) is a person who borrows money when in need, knowing that he cannot repay it as he promises to do. If he cannot be prepared to universalise his situation, then he is not morally justified in promising falsely to repay the money. On the other hand, if he takes into account some extra circumstances then he might be able to justify the action.

Notice that Kant sees the important touchstones as rationality (can you justify it in a rational way) and universality (can you apply it to everyone). But nevertheless, in the end it comes down to the interpretation of moral obligation by the individual. *The implication of this is that each individual constructs, and takes responsibility for, his or her own set of moral values.* Notice that this is very different from the 'natural law' or utilitarian approach.

But notice also that it is a matter of **intention.** The maxim of my action is the principle that lies behind my intention to act in a certain way. That maxim does not depend upon anticipated results, but it does imply certain things about a person's view of the world. Kant argued that, if you respond to an 'ought', you presuppose three things:

- God – because unless there is some guarantor that ultimately doing the right thing will yield the right results, you will not feel committed to behaving in a moral way.

- Freedom – because unless you experience yourself as free, you will have no sense of being able to make a moral choice.

- Immortality – because you know that you may not see the results of all that you do in this life, and therefore presuppose that there is some future life in which the present imbalance of actions and rewards will be rectified.

Kant does not mean that you **have** to believe in these three things in order to respond to an 'ought', but that, once you acknowledge the unconditional nature of that 'ought' it implies that you believe in them.

Not everyone would accept this, for it is based on the idea that there is a rational structure to our thought that underlies our instinctive reactions. This may not be so. We may feel an obligation for the worst of motives, or from unconscious needs. The presuppositions are not necessary – at least not in a conscious sense.

—— THE CREATIVE RESPONSE ——

There is a further point to note here - one to which we will return in the next chapter. For the natural law and utilitarian approaches, we look out at the world and analyze either its structure (if you are looking for purpose) or the likely results of action (if you are a utilitarian). But when a person makes a moral choice, he or she is not merely responding to an external situation, but creating something new – taking an active step to change the world, not merely to respond to the way it is.

This active side of moral choice shapes both external circumstances and the personality of the person who acts – character is shown and developed through such choices. Morality, including the categorical imperative, is therefore a category by which we interpret and change the world. We do not find a 'categorical imperative' out there – it is not a piece of data in the world. To a person who says it does not exist, there is no objective proof to offer. It is not part of the world, but a feature of the way in which a person responds to the world.

Morality is therefore about creative response, about interpreting the world in such a way that we give it value.

Things have value for us, and we are sometimes required to express those values – and choose between conflicting values - value does not inhere in the external object, but in the relationship that I have with it.

An example:

A stamp collector comes across a perfect specimen of a Penny Black: it's maltese cross cancellation is clear and bright crimson; it is a printing from a late plate – making it extra rare for a red cancellation; it has perfectly even and large margins; the cancellation has left the profile clear – in short, to the collector, it is a treasure! To me, it is really just a rather drab bit of paper. It serves no useful purpose. I take it between my fingers, tear it in half and throw it on the fire. It flares up for a moment, but gives little warmth – a thing of no value.

- Value does not inhere in the Penny Black. The collector has created a web of values; the stamp is part of that web. It receives the value that it is given.

If morality depends upon a sense of values, and values do not inhere in objects, but in the relationship between people and objects (or people and one another) then morality is a far more flexible thing than a straight utilitarian (or a follower of 'natural law') might imagine.

Two examples:

In 1993, the Pope issued a encyclical Veritatis Splendor. In it he reaffirmed the church's opposition to, amongst other things, sex outside marriage, homosexuality and

---

masturbation. The basis of this opposition is clear, both in terms of the authority of the Church, and also the rational theology with which that authority is underpinned.

In other words, the encyclical sets out a set of values, and by those values there follows the ruling that certain actions are immoral.

- Those who oppose the encyclical may not actually care for the theological debate on which is it based. They may simply say that their world is one based on very different values, in which sex and human relationships are judged by different criteria.

- Given the basis upon which his morality is based, no doubt the Pope will be judged correct. But some people have a very different set of values, and thus a different morality.

In March 1993, five members of a homosexual ring who enjoyed sado-masochistic acts of genital torture, appealed to the House of Lords against an Appeal Court ruling in 1992 that a court did not have to prove that there was lack of consent in order to convict on charges of unlawful wounding. In other words, if a person taking part in a sado-masochistic act decides to bring a charge against the person who has inflicted pain, that person cannot then defend himself on the grounds that he believed the recipient of the pain was a willing participant at the time.

Here are two of the Law Lords' comments. One said that society was:

> '..entitled and bound to defend itself against a cult of violence. Pleasure derived from the infliction of pain is an evil thing.'

And another, that sado-masochistic homosexual activity was not:

> 'conducive to the enhancement or enjoyment of family life of the welfare of society'.

- Neither comment is particularly surprising, but notice the implications. The statement that pleasure derived from pain is evil is a maxim which can be applied universally. (One might assume, for example, that the Law Lords oppose foxhunting on the same grounds.) On the other hand, from a strictly Kantian point of view, this does not imply that the sado-masochist was, at the time of inflicting the pain, actually going against any personal conviction. He might have welcomed the idea that everyone should be free to enjoy the inflicting of pain. In other words, an individual's values and view of life might make the inflicting of pain morally acceptable if it is considered only from the standpoint of the individual. The Law Lord appears to base his comment on either natural law (what is the purpose of pain?), or possibly on a utilitarian basis, assuming that society as a whole might be affected by the development of such practices, and that not all would regard pain as a pleasure.

- The second comment is again based on natural law. The assumption is that sexuality is about the enhancement of family life. Since homosexual sado-masochism is hardly likely to fulfil that particular criterion, it is seen as wrong. But does that mean that any sexual act that does not do so – nor which promotes the welfare of society – is therefore morally wrong?

These examples highlight the fact that values and commitments are not decided on rational grounds alone. Individuals and groups explore and develop their own criteria for value and therefore for moral judgement. What one group will regard as morally accept- able, another will condemn. We also need to see that a Kantian approach here is essentially individualistic, whereas many deci- sions taken in law, but backed up by moral assertions, are made on the basis of public good or civic duty – and this may sometimes conflict with the wishes of minority groups.

— DETERMINED AND YET FREE? —

Before leaving Kant, let us refer back to the issue with which we were concerned in the second chapter. Kant held that our minds impose space, time and causality on the phenomena that they encounter. From an external point of view, everything is conditioned. When I observe someone else making a choice, my mind naturally seeks out the causes that led to that particular choice. In the world of phenomena, there can be no freedom.

But Kant held that all we know about are the phenomena that come through our senses. We know things as they appear to us, not things as they are in themselves. (Things-in-themselves he calls 'noumena', our perception of them 'phenomena'.)

On this basis, he is able to say that we are, at one and the same time phenomenally conditioned (perceived from the outside, I have no freedom), but also noumenally free (I experience my freedom to act – something which I know, but nobody else can observe).

There are therefore two ways of understanding the moral act – from the standpoint of one who observes the choices that are made, with their consequences and the implications they have for an understanding of humankind, and from the standpoint of the person who is actually confronted with a choice – who in a moment of creative action actually respond to values and convictions and puts them into effect.

– PHILOSOPHERS OR POLITICIANS? –

Kant was a professional philosopher, and by all accounts his life was regular and carefully ordered. There is an anecdote told of him that he took the same walk each day, and that his timing was so precise that housewives, seeing him pass, could set their watches by him! His thought is precise and logical.

• He looked at experience and realised that we play a large part in the ordering of what we see – we impose space, time and causality on the sense impressions which bombard us.

- He looked at the experience of behaving in a moral way, responding to a sense that there is something that one 'ought' to do, and analyzed that too – both in terms of its implications and its presuppositions.

- He presents us with two simple rules: universalisability, and treating people as ends and not as means – both eminently sensible criteria by which to assess our moral choices.

- He does not offer practical advice for specific situations, but the most general of guidelines.

Why then might one hesitate to accept Kant as the ultimate judge of acceptable action? Perhaps because in the actual world of crises and moral decisions, life is seldom as straightforward as it would seem to be from Kant's standpoint.

To get a realistic view of moral choices, we need to balance what we feel 'ought' to happen by a study of what does actually happen. From Kant's perspective much of what happens – especially, perhaps in the world of politics – might be regarded as immoral. But is that fair? Should we not look carefully at the actual choices that people make if they are to rule? Should we not balance the innocent simplicity of the categorical imperative against the experience of one who sees the consequence of always acting innocently?

For a very different perspective, we shall now turn to a politician – a fifteenth century Italian from Florence, a diplomat and shrewd if cynical observer of the realities of political life. His maxims are rather different from those of Kant!

MACHIAVELLI

Machiavelli was essentially a practical man. His book *The Prince* gives advice to one who would seek to rule a principality, and it is set against the political intrigues of 15th and 16th century Italy. It looks at the realities of political life, the need for stern action, the need to use power in a way that is effective, the need to act creatively and decisively, breaking all the conventional moral rules if necessary, in order to deal in a pragmatic way with the demands of high office.

Machiavelli's views are suitable to balance against Kant's for three reasons:

1. Kant is concerned with the 'categorical imperative' – the 'ought' that does not depend upon conditions. Machiavelli is concerned almost all the time with 'hypothetical imperatives' – e.g. what you need to do in order to retain power – and the implication of this is that, in most practical situations, it is the hypothetical rather than the categorical which constitutes the normal sphere of 'moral' (to Machiavelli) operations.

2. Kant argues that you should always treat people as ends, not as means. Machiavelli recognises that there are occasions when a ruler must act cruelly against one person or group of people in order to establish fear as a deterrent against lawlessness, for example. Treating people as ends in themselves, he might well argue, leads to anarchy and chaos.

3. Kant assumes that the right thing to do is judged by what I would wish other people to do. Machiavelli argues that the right thing to do is judged by what I know other people will try to do to me given half a chance.

Let us look at just a little of Machiavelli's advice:

Here, for example, is his advice to a ruler who has taken over a state. (But it might equally apply to a Managing Director who has taken over an ailing company, or a politician inheriting a new Ministry.)

'So it should be noted that when he seizes a state the new ruler ought to determine all the injuries that he will need to inflict. He should inflict them once for all, and not have to renew them every day, and in that way he will be able to set men's minds at rest, and win them over to him when he confers benefits. Whoever acts otherwise, either through timidity or bad advice, is always forced to have the knife ready in his hand and he can never depend on his subjects because they, suffering fresh and continuous violence, can never feel secure with regard to him. Violence should be inflicted once for all; people will then forget what it tastes like and so be less resentful. Benefits should be conferred gradually; and in that way they will taste better.'

(*The Prince*, section VIII)

Like a surgeon, forced in some extreme circumstances to operate without anaesthetic, one may sometimes be in a position where the inflicting of pain is inevitable and ultimately beneficial.

It might seem irrelevant to ask, 'I am prepared for everyone to operate without anaesthetics?' because clearly the actual decision is not based on a general theory, but on the immediate and unique situation. The surgeon might say 'This is not how I would choose to act, but in the circumstances it is right for me to do so.' What Machiavelli is saying (and using a utilitarian argument to justify it) is that less harm will be done by decisive action than by a compassionate but indecisive muddle.

And here the advice to a ruler might be adapted for a new teacher, taking over an unruly class:

'So a prince should not worry if he incurs reproach for his cruelty so long as he keeps his subjects united and loyal. By making an example or two he will prove more compassionate than those who, being too compassionate, allow disorders which lead to murder and rapine. These nearly always harm the whole community, whereas executions ordered by a prince only affect individuals.'

(*The Prince*, section XVIII)

He acknowledges the traditional virtues, but comments:

'... taking everything into account, he (the prince) will find that some of the things that appear to be virtues will, if he practises them, ruin him, and some of the things that appear to be wicked will bring him security and prosperity.'

(*The Prince*, section XV)

Examples of this follow. He recognises that it is praiseworthy for a prince to honour his word, and be straightforward rather than crafty in his dealings, but sometimes it is necessary to break one's word, if keeping it means placing himself at a disadvantage. His reasoning for this is clear:

> 'If all men were good, this precept would not be good; but because men are wretched creatures who would not keep their word to you, you need not keep your word to them.'

So that:

> '.. he should have a flexible disposition, varying as fortune and circumstances dictate. As I said above, he should not deviate from what is good, if that is possible, but he should know how to do evil, if that is necessary.'

> (*The Prince*, section XVIII)

Overall, he takes this view of the relationship between ruler and ruled:

> 'From this (that a prince's behaviour should be tempered by humanity) arises the following question: whether it is better to be loved than feared, or the reverse. The answer is that one would like to be both the one and the other; but because it is difficult to combine them, it is far better to be feared than loved if you cannot be both.'

> (*The Prince*, section XVII)

For our purposes, there are four features of Machiavelli's advice that we may need to take into account:

1. In many situations, traditional virtues may be set aside, and actions judged on a utilitarian basis. Keeping order and minimising pain take precedence over traditional moral principles.

2. Actions depend upon the duties and responsibilities of the particular position that I hold in society. A prince might be justified, therefore, in doing something which would not be acceptable in one of his subjects. Once you have accepted the

position of ruler, you are obliged to see the benefit and integrity of the state – your morality in other respects being subsumed beneath that overall obligation. Morality is therefore related to social position.

3. In practical terms, one needs to be flexible, adapting moral principles to suit particular situations.

4. What we do should depend on our awareness of the likely actions and attitudes of those around us. If everyone else were good, there would be no problem, but they aren't, and so we remain naively innocent at our own peril.

An example:

From a British Government Defence White Paper, published April 2nd 1993, concerning the retention of a nuclear deterrent in spite of the emergence of democracy within the Warsaw Pact countries:

'We do not, for example, particularly expect that the democratic reforms in Eastern Europe will fail – we do not want them to fail. But the business of defence is to be ready to give protection... Defence arrangements therefore cannot sensibly be made the leading agent of political change, the instrument through which Western nations express their best hopes and happiest aspirations. It makes no sense accordingly to throw away safeguards simply because we would like not to need them any more.'
(from an article, Defence White Paper, *The Independant*, April 3rd 1990)

With these sentiments, Machiavelli would be the first to agree. Prudent defence of the state is regarded as overriding personal or moral feelings about the destructive power of armaments. Machiavelli would have condemned the Campaign for Nuclear Disarmament on the grounds that the risks involved with disarming would threaten the welfare of the state.

The ultimate choice -

There is, of course, an answer to Machiavelli – but it is not an easy one. One could say:

> 'I will do what I know to be right, no matter what the consequences, to myself, my family and friends, my country. I will not compromise my integrity, however much pain that might cause.'

That is a valid moral position to take, for someone who holds his or her principles very dear. Martyrs take such a stand.

It is also possible to take that position for quite other reasons: out of fear of being in the wrong; out of pride or stubbornness; out of the conviction that future glory awaits those who stand by their principles (either in heaven, in a new incarnation, or in the perspective of history). As T S Eliot put onto the lips of the soon-to-be-martyred Thomas à Becket in his play *Murder in the Cathedral*, when Thomas is tempted to accept martyrdom for the sake of future glory, that the foulest treason is to do the right thing for the wrong reason.

Let Machiavelli stand for those who are sceptical about the application of moral principles. This is not a total scepticism about moral values, which implies that there are no values other than those that individuals choose to impose on life. It is just a scepticism about the application of general rules to individual situations.

In almost all moral systems, there is scope for individual flexibility. In extreme circumstances you are morally justified in doing things that would be wrong in the general run of events.

Machiavelli takes this seriously, but in political life almost all events are extreme and unique, all demand that normal rules be set aside. Just how flexible can people be before they are 'unprincipled'? Is Machiavelli really unprincipled, or just a realist, applying moral guidelines as best he may in the world of political survival?

—— A SUMMARY ——

How far have we come in our exploration of 'The Art of Living'?

We started by examining if we were actually free to make choices and act on them.

- We then asked what we meant by moral statements – Did they describe something objective, or just our feelings? Did they seek to have an effect on the hearers – actually to recommend a course of action? How might they be shown to be true or false?

- We then started the quest for a suitable basis upon which we could decide what is right and wrong. The first to be considered was 'natural law' – that everything in the universe has a purpose, and that the fulfilling of it constitutes its 'good'. We noted that it is not universally agreed that there is such a purpose, nor how it can be applied to individual actions. We also saw that following 'natural law' was not the same thing as being natural.

- We then turned to utilitarianism – the examination of the expected results of an action. But we found that results were neither unambiguous nor complete, and that there were many different ways in which they could be assessed. Predicting and weighing results was likely to be a long process, and one which might well lead to the permanent postponement of any decision.

- We therefore looked at the experience of moral obligation – the 'ought' of Kant's categorical imperative – and against it set the down-to-earth scepticism of one who is forced to adapt morality to suit the demands of survival in a generally immoral world.

Where do we go from here?

Moral choices show the freedom to act in a way which reflects a person's convictions and values. Without such convictions and values, morality would make no sense – there would be no reason to choose to do one thing rather than another.

A sceptic could say 'There is no way to prove that anything is either right or wrong. There are no objective moral values. Everyone is free to do whatever he or she chooses'. But that does not really get away from the issue of values, for even the sceptic must make choices based on something – personal survival or comfort, perhaps.

Moral choices and moral values operate within different spheres of life – the personal, the social, the global and the religious. Each of these is like an observation platform, since each gives us a particular viewpoint from which to survey the world, its values and its choices.

The platforms are:

1. Personal development – both for yourself and others

2. Society – its laws and the way in which it functions

3. The global perspective on moral issues – those things that involve humankind as a whole, other species and care of the planet

4. The values that come from religious experience and the traditions of the world's major religions.

Which platform you choose at any one time may depend upon your circumstances.

- A therapist is likely to evaluate a client's 'art of living' primarily on the basis of his or her personal development.

- A judge or politician is likely to evaluate it in terms of what is socially acceptable or possible.

- A conservationist, politician, or someone concerned with animal rights, may sometimes ask what the global implications of a particular course of action might be, or how we should treat other species.

- A religious believer, irrespective of prevailing secular trends, is likely to follow the guidelines of his or her faith, using its values to aid the process of moral choice.

These platforms are not mutually exclusive, we may operate within all of them from time to time. So, for example, from the social platform one person might be asking about the rights and responsibilities that can be expected of a citizen, whilst, in the same debate, another may be asking in what way society should be ordered to enable each person to develop his or her potential. The values and priorities of the two viewpoints might well be different.

Conflict between the views from each of these platforms is the stuff of literature – films, books and plays thrive on it – as well as moral debate.

Illustrations:

Reflect on, or scan the reviews of plays, books or films. Notice any of the following features:

- Conflict between personal longing and social order (plenty of historical fiction here), where a person breaks out of a social straightjacket.

- Conflict between social order and religious conviction (one could start, perhaps with the T S Eliot's *Murder in the Cathedral* mentioned previously, *A Man for all Seasons* about Thomas More, biographies of the Dalai Lama ...)

- Conflict between duty to one's own society or nation and a wider, global responsibility (Plenty of thrillers have combined this with the personal element – an individual

---

is caught between the demands of his government and perceived global dangers of some new weapon or research, along with a love affair which offers personal happiness while transcending political barriers and loyalties.)

- Conflict between personal, emotional fulfilment and a religious vocation (A few years ago Coleen McCullough's bestselling novel *The Thorn Birds*, explored this – but there are many others.)

Moral integrity is very much a matter of reconciling and balancing the various platforms from which we have to operate, and the values that they offer us. Within the parameters of each platform, we may evaluate choices from the standpoint of natural law, of utilitarianism, or the categorical imperative.

Within them we may ask if we are really free to make a moral choice, and whether their values imply moral relativism (in which there are no objective moral standards) or absolute moral rules.

7

—— PERSONAL ——
DEVELOPMENT

Before the 16th century, moral thinking was dominated by the influence of Aristotle, mediated through Christian theologians, of whom Aquinas was the most influential. It was heavily dependent upon the authority of religion and of the Church. With the Reformation and the intellectual upheavals that followed, that authoritarian structure was replaced by the desire to find a rational basis for action. From the 17th and 18th centuries we find the development of two lines of approach to ethics. One is utilitarianism, the other idealism – represented respectively by Mill and by Kant.

Both were dependent, in one way or another, on the values of the older 'natural law' view of the universe. Utilitarianism falls back on values, as it seeks to say what constitutes happiness, or the good of the greatest number. Kant, on the other hand, having come to the conclusion that you could not prove God, freedom or immortality by examining the phenomena of the world, decided that he should reinstate them as *presuppositions* of the practical reason – as the assumptions that lay behind all morality.

To a certain extent, these assumptions have continued to be featured in moral thinking right through to the present day. Intuitionism, which we looked at in Chapter 3, argued that there were certain things that could be known by intuition, but not explained. 'Goodness', known intuitively, is rather like Kant's idea of God being a presupposition of one's moral experience, it is just there in the background, without which nothing makes sense.

But what if we set this tradition aside and explore values that are not found 'out there' in a general understanding of the world, but ones we create for ourselves as we act and make choices? Can we create values, as an artist creates an abstract picture, rather than discover them, as a photographer might record a beautiful but external scene? Can we, as individuals, stop **asking** what is right, and start **deciding what will be** right?

This will be an important question as we look at moral choice from the standpoint of the human individual and his or her personal development. But first of all, it is important to recognise that such development takes place in a social context; so how does personal development relate to the way in which we treat other people?

ALTRUISM?

Can human beings act genuinely for the benefit of others?

Thomas Hobbes, in *Leviathan* (1651), argued that, if people voluntarily give up their rights for the benefit of others, they do so in order to achieve something good for themselves. Indeed, he claimed that every voluntary act had as its aim some good to be obtained for oneself. On this basis, although the benefit done to oneself may be less tangible than the benefit offered to the other person (e.g. feeling good for having been charitable), nevertheless, in some way we are all fundamentally concerned primarily with ourselves.

By contrast, Hume's *Enquiry Concerning the Principles of Morals* (1751) takes the view that people do actually experience 'sympathy' – that is, they respond when they see the suffering or the joy of others. He makes this experience basic to his ethics, in that if there were no sympathy then there would be no development of altruistic qualities.

This does not mean that people respond to the sufferings of others in a generous way all the time, but that everyone can experience some degree of sympathy. A psychopath, for example, is someone who has no sense of right or wrong, and who is not going to be persuaded by reason, but has urges (to kill, for example) that are totally devoid of any sense of sympathy for his or her victim. In other words, for the psychopath, other people are treated as 'things', not as fellow human beings who have feelings, and to whom one might want to relate in a personal way. In this case, the exception illustrates the general rule – that people are capable of responding to the sufferings of others.

Hume also holds that people can exhibit qualities that both give happiness to themselves and are also useful to others. These 'virtues' include justice, faithfulness and politeness, which are not directly related to self-development or happiness, but to the interests of others. In fact, Hume regards *benevolence* as the highest quality of which human nature is capable.

Now, such virtues are qualities that a person can develop. In this sense, altruism is a sign of personal development. But this is very different from a personal development that is done for selfish reasons, and at the expense of other people.

In section 9 of the *Enquiry*... Hume seems to step back from saying that sympathy is always its own justification. He points out that, even if someone appears to lose out personally because of some action for the benefit of others, nevertheless he or she will feel inner peace of mind and satisfaction, which leads to personal happiness. Notice that Hume is not saying that one should show sympathy **because** it leads to peace of mind, but that peace of mind happens to be a result of the genuine response of sympathy. (Unlike Hobbes, who seems to be saying that sympathy is merely disguised self-love.)

So, in assessing personal development as a feature of morality we need to reflect on three possibilities:

1. That people are basically selfish, and if they are honest they will admit it.

2. That people think they are unselfish and considerate to others, but, in fact, they are really just satisfying their own deeper needs.

3. That people can genuinely feel and respond to the situations of others, and can show qualities of honest altruism.

There is one other important feature of Hume's idea of 'sympathy' to keep in mind. When we looked at Aristotle in Chapter 4, we saw that he attempted to give some objective criterion for moral statements. His idea of what was right stemmed from reason, and an intellectual conception about the purpose of human existence. Hume, by contrast, has no such rational basis for his morality. It is not based on intellectual argument, but on experience. In this respect, it is parallel to Kant's *categorical imperative* which is understood only in the moment of being aware of a moral demand.

If a person is to develop, that development takes place within a social context – in other words, personal development implies personal worth in terms of relationships. It would be difficult to develop personally in total isolation from others; and even (as, for example, through some form of religious asceticism) if a person could achieve a high degree of personal growth in isolation, it would still depend upon the religious and social ideas that set up the conditions for that growth in the first place. This social context was emphasised by F H Bradley in an essay called 'My station and its duties' (in *Ethical Studies* 1876). He argued that self-realisation was the basis of ethics, and he followed the philosopher Hegel in pointing out that people need self-expression and also recognition if they are to enjoy the good life. That recognition can come through the family relationships, through the local society, or through the state, since (according to Hegel) these are the basic spheres of influence.

- Central to Bradley (and Hegel) is the idea that self-realisation (achieving one's full potential as a unique human being) is not something to be examined in isolation, but is a feature of society. As we look at claims that freedom for the individual is of fundamental importance, because it allows autonomy and personal development, we need to remember that this always takes place in a social context. One person's freedom may well curtail the freedom of another.

NIETZSCHE

The thinker who most radically challenged traditional moral thinking and placed human development at the centre of a value creating system of thought was Friedrich Nietzsche.

It is often valuable to consider a thinker's work against the background of his or her personal circumstances, although with many philosophers this is discouraged by the way that they present ideas in a cogent fashion, inviting logical comment only. Nietzsche is different. His writing is vivid, and his ideas are sometimes presented as images. It may be worth reflecting therefore that he was born in 1844, the son of a Lutheran pastor, and of the daughter of a country vicar, and that as a young man he was both a lover of solitude, enthusiastically religious, and also highly talented. (He composed a motet at the age of 10, and by 14 had written some fifty poems, and had decided that he wanted to be a writer.)

We shall approach Nietzsche's work through four key features.

The first of these is the idea that 'God is Dead'. Remember, this is not a casual comment from one who has not taken religious seriously, it is a conclusion about the state of things as Nietzsche saw them in the 1880s. In *The Joyous Science* he has the image of a madman who comes into the town with the message that 'God is Dead'. Not that God had never existed, but that people had killed him. He asks if his hearers do not sense that it is growing darker, that they need lamps, even at noon. He tries to explain that people have cut the world loose, and that (without God) it is wandering without fixed values and without direction.

This is perhaps the most stark recognition of what had taken place, almost since the Reformation: the replacement of the authoritarian and metaphysical structure of thought by the elevation of human reason. Whatever they may claim to believe, people in fact measure and create values based on themselves, not on God. They are the centre and measure of life.

It is presented, not as something good or bad, but as an observation – something that he is amazed others have not realised.

The next feature is the Superman (a rather poor translation of Ubermensch, which means something that goes over or beyond man). In *Thus Spoke Zarathustra*, the sage Zarathustra comes down his mountain. He opens his teaching by saying:

> 'I teach you the Superman. Man is something that should be overcome. What have you done to overcome him?

> All creatures hitherto have created something beyond themselves: and do you want to be the ebb of this great tide, and return to the animals rather than overcoming man?'

> (trans Hollingdale, Penguin, p41)

Here the context is evolution. As the ape is to humankind, so humankind will be to the Superman.

He then takes an important step:

> 'The Superman is the meaning of the earth. Let your will say: The Superman *shall be* the meaning of the earth!'

In other words, from this moment on humankind is to choose its values and its direction by an act of will. We humans are to be the creators of value. He is critical of those who sought some heavenly goal, accusing them of being poisoners, weakening mankind. Instead, the true goal is to be in the future, the Ubermensch. It is an affirmation of life, and of the human will which shapes and determines that life.

The third feature is 'the will to power', which is the force behind his moral thinking. It does not mean a crude attempt to get power, but the affirmation of life, and the will to develop and move forward. It is the will to power that, for Nietzsche, is the source of all values, and therefore the source of morality.

Nietzsche's thought is highly individualistic. Wanting to be equal with others and showing humility – key features of democracy and Christianity, as he sees them – are a sign of decadence and weakness. They sap the will to power and desire for personal development. For this reason, Nietzsche opposed both democracy and Christianity. According to Nietzsche, exploitation is one of the basic features of life, and self development is fundamental. Therefore we should be free to adopt whatever means we want in order to secure that power. In *Beyond Good and Evil,* he sees the world as divided into masters and slaves, and he holds that the morality that suits the one will not suit the other. Masters are free to do what their own creative development requires. Nietzsche rejects both democracy and Christianity because they are associated with slave values, not with master values. Both democracy and Christianity cause the decay of the state, because they are based on the false assumption that all are equal. He attacks Christianity because it allows people to deny themselves on earth for the sake of God and a heavenly reward.

This is perhaps where it is important to recognise Nietzsche's background in 19th century protestantism. Not everyone taking a religious position today would view Christian values in quite the way he did. Nevertheless it is true that some moral principles emphasise humility and co-operation, others stress personal development and the competitive spirit. Nietzsche's is one of the latter.

Finally, there is 'the eternal recurrence'. This is a difficult and complex idea. Perhaps it may be approached by contrasting it with the ideas of Aristotle or traditional Christian views. In Aristotle, everything has an end or a purpose. It achieves its goal once it fulfils that end. The world looks to something outside itself to justify its existence. In the traditional Christian scheme, this is God. But for Nietzsche, God is dead. There is no way that this present life can be simply tolerated because it leads to or points to something beyond itself. One should therefore be prepared to accept life as it is. To affirm it and work with it.

His graphic way of presenting this idea is to speak of accepting that everything that happens will be repeated over and over again. Can you can look at such an endlessly repeating life and still affirm it? Can you enjoy it just as it is, without asking for some external compensation or explanation? Nietzsche presents a challenge – a necessary challenge in any world that has consciously or unconsciously discarded religious belief and the old metaphysics that went with it. The challenge of 'the eternal recurrence' is to accept life as it is.

Nietzsche's writings are a challenge, and these notes hardly touch the surface of what he has to say on the topic of morality.

They are included here because Nietzsche looks at morality in a way that is quite different from the older 'natural law' and 'utilitarian' arguments. He takes the platform of personal development and makes it central to morality.

> **A *point for reflection*:**
>
> Through the 'will to power', one should 'give style' to one's character and the greatest enjoyment is 'to live dangerously!' In *Beyond Good and Evil*, Nietzsche said of morality:
>
> > 'Every morality is a rationalisation of fear, a set of safety instructions on how to live at peace with the most dangerous aspects of one's self.'
>
> - What might a modern psychologist make of this?
> - How is it possible to be afraid of aspects of oneself, or to regard oneself as dangerous?
> - What might be the ethical implication of admitting that, consciously or unconsciously, we have a 'will to power' and that it is the source of our values?

— NIETZSCHE AND MACHIAVELLI —

Before leaving Nietzsche, let us refer back to the section on Machiavelli at the end of the last chapter.

Machiavelli was contrasted with Kant. The one was giving practical advice about how to survive the political intrigues of 15th century Italy, the other was thinking highly abstract thoughts in 18th century Germany. The question there was whether the generalised ideals of the categorical imperative outlined by Kant could actually be applied in the realities of life, or whether – like the earlier Machiavelli – one should aim to survive by being free to break all conventional laws where necessary.

Nietzsche has presented a similar challenge. Both he and Machiavelli refer to Cesare Borgia – one of the most ruthless contemporaries of Machiavelli – with some degree of approval. He exemplified qualities of strength, and was a skilled political operator.

- Machiavelli argues that, for political survival and the integrity of the principality over which you rule, you cannot afford the luxury of always keeping your word, or treating others fairly. There are occasions when you have to rule by fear, to prevent social and political chaos.

- Nietzsche would call this 'master morality' as oppose to the weakening, protective 'slave morality'.

There are questions that we might put to these thinkers:

- (to Machiavelli) Why should political survival and the integrity of the state be accepted as the overall criterion by which political action is judged? Where does that value come from?

- (to Nietzsche) Why should I express a 'will to power'? Why should I want to overcome myself and become something greater? If there is no external guarantee of values, why should I be forced to adopt my own personal development as the supreme value?

An example:

'Suicide is not exclusive to humans and lemmings – cells kill themselves too. Cells do away with themselves surprisingly often during the normal development and adult life of many animals. How do they do it? Suicidal cells shrink, chew up their own DNA – which contains their hereditary information – and feed themselves to their neighbours. It's all over within a hour or two.

'It is because some cells kill themselves and others survive that, for example, fingers are sculptured on an embryo's hand from a solid mass of cells, a mother's womb clears a space for the baby to plug into her blood supply, and mutant cells self-destruct before they have a chance to become cancerous. So not only do cells kill themselves, but it is important that they do.'

(From an article by Harriet Coles 'The death that is essential to life', *The Daily Telegraph*, July 19th 1993)

- If it is natural and necessary for some cells to commit suicide, is it not also natural that some people should sacrifice themselves for the sake of others?

- If so, is it not unrealistic to expect personal development to be the only criterion of morality? Perhaps, in order for society to survive, there should be, if not a 'slave morality', then at least a co-operative morality? A world filled with aspiring Cesare Borgias is unlikely to be a happy one for all concerned!

OTHER APPROACHES

In terms of personal development, there are two other thinkers we should consider here. They have had enormous influences on modern ethics – and both of them look to self-realisation of the individual as a criterion in evaluating their theories.

• Marx

Marx saw the suffering of the proletariat in the way in which the wage labourer was separated off from the product of his labours. He could no longer get pride or personal satisfaction from his work. He was simply a function in a process from which someone else made a profit. This Marx called 'alienation'.

Whatever the practical consequences of Marx's thought, we should at least acknowledge this fundamental problem of aliena-tion – that creativity, and the ability to benefit from one's own labours are part of what it means to be a happy, fulfilled person. To be alienated in work is to cut off from one's personal sphere a large part of life.

• Freud

In his analysis of the self, Freud introduced a threefold division – the id, the ego and the super-ego – of these, the super-ego was the 'conscience', source of moral commands, taken in as rules during childhood and now (for those who are psychologically unhealthy) unconsciously inhibiting the free expression of the rational self, the ego. For health, according to most psychological theories, the ego needs to be in control. Health is the freedom to understand one's needs and wants, to see how one might develop to achieve them, and to take steps in that direction, free from neurotic guilt. All that takes personal development as its criterion of health.

There is far more that both Marx and Freud could contribute to our study of ethics, but for now it is only important to recognise that they both emphasise this central feature of personal development. They also follow Nietzsche in seeing the moral self as creating something positive, and not just responding to circumstances. Marx sought to change the world, rather than simply to understand it, and psychotherapy seeks to set clients free from all that inhibits the natural flowering of their personality.

— SOME PERSONAL VALUES AND — CHOICES

A central question for us is this:

• Is it possible (or necessary) to take personal development of the individual as a basis for making moral judgments and choices, and for developing the values which those judgements and choices express?

To explore this, we shall now turn to a number of moral issues, asking what implications they have for personal development.

CHOOSING THE SEX OF A BABY

'Choosing babies' sex is unethical, say doctors'
' Treatment to enable parents to choose the sex of their baby in advance was declared unethical – unless there were compelling medical reasons for doing so – by the British Medical Association yesterday.

'Doctors received the go-ahead to practise sex selection for medical reasons but it was ruled out for purely "social reasons".'

One consultant argued that:

'..it was acceptable for parents to be given a choice when in-vitro fertilisation methods produced embryos of both sexes'

adding that:

'if treatment resulted in five male and five female embryos, there was no reason for doctors to shuffle them and implant three at random. There was nothing unethical in such circumstances in letting parents choose which embryos they wanted implanting.'

In reply, another consultant said:

'.. the method would be used by people who, for religious reasons, wanted boys rather than girls. That was "totally intoler-able",' adding 'There will be pressure on doctors ... to create more male babies. To perpetuate that sort of society does not seem ethical at all'.'

[From an article by David Fletcher, *The Daily Telegraph* June 30th 1993]

- Notice how these doctors use the word 'ethical'. They assume that a choice is 'ethical' if it follows from an accepted set of moral norms, and therefore unethical if it transgresses them. Their problem is that they are using different starting points in their assessment of the situation.

- The first doctor seems to be basing her argument on the idea that individuals should be able to develop themselves (and their offspring, in this case) as they wish, with medical help, provided that this development and choice does not harm others.

- The second doctor uses a very different argument. He starts with the assumption of equality of the sexes – and the benefit therefore of ridding society of those things which tend towards discrimination. He then notes that some religious beliefs encourage inequality. Finding a conflict between these two sets of values, he opts for the first and calls the second unethical.

- It is worth noting that the second doctor is not actually referring to a religious attitude at all, but a social one, held by members of a particular ethnic minority, who also happen to be members of a particular religion. This is important, because the choice is not one between religious values and a social ideal, but between two differing social ideals.

Some issues raised by this:

- Should individual freedom (to choose the sex of a child) be limited by social theory?

- Should a minority have their ideals overruled by a majority?

- If a doctor 'cheated' on this British Medical Association ruling and used more female embryos than male, knowing that the parents wanted to have a female child, against whose interests would he or she be acting? The unborn child's? The parents'? Society's?

What arguments are being used here?

- The first doctor is using 'personal development' as a primary value to be taken into account. People should be free to develop themselves and their families as they wish.

- The second might be using a utilitarian argument:

  It is in the interests of a majority of people in society if equality of the sexes is established. The decision to give birth to more boys than girls reflects sex prejudice. Therefore is it wrong.

  Equally, it could follow from natural law:

  There is a natural balance between males and females in society. That is achieved by the random selection of fertilised embryos for natural implantation in the womb. Artificial selection of such embryos may frustrate a balance of nature by interfering with that process.

Notice, however, that selection is allowed on medical grounds

(e.g. to prevent the continuation of genetically transmitted diseases; muscular dystrophy, for example, affects only boys.)

- In this case, the absolute rule that a doctor is to seek to promote health and cure or prevent disease, takes precedence over both the social and ethnic preferences, and also over the principle that parents should be free to choose the sex of their offspring. It would generally be accepted on this basis that it would be wrong for a doctor to allow selection of a particular sex knowing that the choice would probably result in the birth of a child carrying a genetic disease.

SEX AND PERSONAL DEVELOPMENT

It is a caricature of medieval society to say that the sexual act was often one expressing power and property rather than love, or even straightforward lust. Nevertheless, it is true that for many societies and for much of history, the legitimate expression of sexuality has been controlled by social norms, including the stability of family life (requiring sex to be confined to marriage partners), the prohibition of homosexuality, and also the use of marriage as a means of forging political, financial or social links between families or even nations.

The history of sexuality need not concern us here, except to point out that, in modern debates about sexuality, there are at least three different ethical approaches:

1. The 'natural law' approach, as exemplified particularly by the views of the Catholic Church. Here, sex has a particular function – the procreation of children. Other uses of sex (as outlined once again in a papal encyclical in 1993) are wrong.

   This view tends to see the sexual act itself as objectively either right or wrong. Sexual orientation, if it does not lead to specific sexual acts, is a different matter. Commenting in July 1993 on discussions on whether the age of consent for homosexual sex should be lowered, Cardinal Hume is reported to have said that while homosexual acts are 'objectively wrong' they (homosexuals) should not feel guilty about their sexual orientation. The Vatican speaks of homosexuality as a 'disorder', but that should not imply a sinful situation or even a sickness.

Notice an implication of this distinction. A homosexual relationship, in the sense of an emotional attachment between two people of the same sex, is not itself sinful. This means that, if you take personal development and fulfilment as a criterion of morality, then there is nothing wrong with homosexuality. The only debate is between those of the 'natural law' view, who see specific acts of homosexual sex as wrong, and those who – examining mainly the relationship and its implications – judge it as they would a heterosexual one. In this case, the actual nature of the sexual acts being considered less important than the emotional commitment and affection that they express.

2. The second main approach is that of utilitarianism.

   • Contraception is advised – to avoid unwanted pregnancy, which in turn is presented as a situation likely to lead to unhappiness, either through abortion or through motherhood, for someone not ready or able to take on that commitment.

   • Condoms are advised – to avoid pregnancy and HIV infection.

   • Agony columns in magazines are full of utilitarian advice – 'if you do X, the likely consequence will be Y'. This is moral advice based on the experience of results.

3. What people increasingly describe as the criterion for embarking on a sexual relationship is the quest for a relationship which is mutually fulfilling, one that enables both partners to grow as individuals through their contact with one another. Sex is seen in that context – as a pleasure in itself, but also as a way of becoming intimate with the partner, sharing in a way that has an effect on the relationship as a whole.

Of these three approaches, it is the third that would seem to be increasingly the one which is used to justify the establishment or break up of a relationship.

The image of the bored and depressed housewife, whose life is stunted through a relationship that offers her no personal fulfilment, has been the starting point of books and films.

Equally, the middleaged man, sexually attracted to a younger women, finds that he starts to take new interest in his appearance. Conventional values by which he has lived for years are discarded; by falling helplessly in love, he also discovers things about himself.

These vignettes are not in themselves the subject matter of ethical debate – although, fleshed out with details, they can indeed become so – but they illustrate the fact that in many spheres of modern Western society, the criterion used for the assessment of sexuality and marriage is that of personal development, and of self-discovery and renewed energy and self-confidence through a fulfilling relationship.

The fact that personal development, particularly for women, can become an important touchstone of sexuality illustrates changes in society. Sexual behaviour can become intertwined with sexism, i.e. the belief that one sex is superior to the other. There have been, and still are, societies in which a wife is regarded as the property of her husband. In Britain, until 1882, women had no control over their own property or money once they were married. What does this sort of control and power do to the physical side of sexual relationships? Power, independence, and control over fertility have made sexuality a much more balanced thing between men and women, and have allowed personal development to be viewed as a realistic expectation of the sexual relationship.

DIVORCE

The same three approaches are taken in discussions about divorce. Where there is a fixed view of the nature of marriage and of family life, then marriages may be seen as dissoluble. In the eyes of the Catholic church, a marriage can only by ended if it can be shown never to have been a valid marriage in the first place.

In the practicalities of divorce, division of property and proper care of any children of the marriage are examined from a utilitarian standpoint – seeking to minimise pain, if not actually to promote happiness.

But the acceptance of divorce on the grounds of 'the irretrievable breakdown of the marriage', rather than because of some particular 'fault' on the part of one or other of the partners, implies that it is the future (or lack of it) for this particular relationship which constitutes the basis for divorce, and it is this which is assessed in the course of marriage counselling.

ABORTION

A newspaper article on abortion began thus:

> 'To some, it is a basic matter of women's rights. To others – their implacable opponents – it is a human rights issue first and foremost. In this debate, there is no meeting of minds, no middle ground, no consensus to edge towards. Only different sets of arguments that run alongside each other and never meet.'
>
> [From an article by Paul Goodman, *The Sunday Telegraph*,
> April 4th 1993]

Of all the ethical issues which people face today, abortion is probably the one that most clearly illustrates the contrasting bases upon which moral judgements are made. The facts are not in doubt, the arguments have been presented time and again, and yet there is no consensus view – indeed, as the newspaper article quoted above implies, no consensus is possible.

The issue of abortion can be approached logically, or pragmatically, or from the standpoint of the personal, physical and emotional needs of the woman who seeks the abortion. It can be seen as an intensely personal issue, or one which is a touchstone for the protection of human rights throughout society. On one side, it is a woman's right to have an abortion, on the other it is the first step towards compulsory euthanasia, selective breeding and a wholesale denial of the uniqueness of each human person and his or her consequent rights.

Let us start by reviewing some of the facts, as they were given in the above newspaper article:

* In Britain in 1991, there were 167,376 abortions

- 95 per cent of the aborted foetuses were healthy
- Since it was legalised in Britain in 1967, there have been about 3 million abortions
- 66 per cent of the women who have abortions are single

The law requires that the agreement of two doctors be given for a pregnancy to be terminated. Abortion can be legally permitted if the foetus is seriously defective, if the risk to the health of the mother from having the child is considered greater than the risk of the termination, and if the birth of the child would have a seriously damaging effect, taking into account the psychological and social situation of the mother and other members of the family.

Abortions can take place (according to British law) up to 24 weeks after conception. However, they can be performed up until birth if there is a risk that the mother will be permanently injured by continuing with the pregnancy, or if the child is seriously handicapped.

AN ANTI-ABORTION ARGUMENT:

Both the ancient Greeks and Romans killed weak or deformed babies by exposing them to the elements. This was justified ethically by both Plato and Aristotle on the grounds that death was to be preferred to a stunted life.

Christianity opposed this, on the grounds that each person had an eternal soul, and was made in the image of God. The decision about when a person should die was to be left to God alone. The crucial question was therefore: When does human life start? If the foetus has a 'soul' then it should be protected.

St Augustine thought that the foetus was 'animated' (received its soul) 60 or 80 days after conception. English law originally followed this principle, and distinguished between abortions before and after 'quickening' – the time when a mother might feel the movement of the child within her.

Modern writers on medical ethics (e.g. B Haring in *Medical Ethics*) tend to point out that at the moment of conception, when the ovum is fertilised, a unique genetic code is fixed, which will determine the characteristics of the individual. Does this mean that a 'person' should be considered to exist – and therefore protected and given rights – from that moment?

A problem – twins:

There are three stages at which the tiny bundle of cells that may become a future human being may instead divide and produce two or more individuals:

1. It can happen on about the 4th or 5th day after conception – this is at about the 8th cell division. In this case, each twin will go on to develop its own placenta.

2. It can happen around the time when the bundle of cells becomes implanted in the womb. In this case, the twins will have the same placenta, and may be identical.

3. It may happen at about the 12th or 14th day, by which time the resulting twins will have to share the same amniotic sac, and may be joined ('siamese twins').

- The genetic code is established at conception. But at any stage through until about the 14th day, one could not say whether that genetic code was going to result in a single or multiple birth.

- Is it therefore reasonable to say that there is a unique human person before the possibility of twins forming?

- There are cases of cells dividing to form twins, and then, during this early stage, coming together again to result in a single birth. If each is an individual with rights from the moment of conception, does this mean that the surviving foetus is guilty of murder? Cannibalism, indeed, if it has absorbed another human individual into itself?

This situation highlights the problem of taking genetic identity as the unquestioned basis of human individuality.

The problem over the separation of twins does not preclude the idea that following conception there should be respect for (or even human rights given to) an embryo, but it raises questions about exactly when human identity is established.

In Britain (following the 1991 Human Fertilisation and Embryology Act) the age limit for abortions was lowered to 24 weeks (except in exceptional circumstances, where the health of the mother is seriously threatened). In the USA the Supreme Court decision of 1973 set the time limit for abortions at 6 months.

The general recognition here is that it is wrong to kill a foetus if it is capable of surviving independently. At this point, it receives the right of protection as a separate human being.

The point made by the anti-abortionists is that such right of protection should be extended back to the earliest stages of conception.

It could be argued that many pregnancies are terminated naturally, which might make an abortion an 'elected miscarriage', and therefore there is no reason why an individual foetus should be protected. But this argument is not logical. Human beings are being killed naturally all the time. If I stab someone through the heart, I cannot plead in my defence that many people suffer sudden cardiac arrest, and that I am simply electing that the person should die in that particular way. To induce a cardiac arrest is an action for which I would be morally responsible. To terminate the life of a foetus is also an action for which moral responsibility should be taken, irrespective of whether or not nature might have done the same thing.

Those who oppose abortion also point out that, once life is devalued at one particular point, then all life is under threat. They may present abortion as a touchstone for assessing issues like involuntary euthanasia, or even eugenics (selective breeding). Once the principle is established that it is legally and morally acceptable to destroy life in one particular, then life in general is threatened.

THE PRO-FREEDOM ARGUMENT

This argument is not presented as pro-abortion, because very few people would actually choose to have an abortion. It is not regarded as a 'good' to be sought, but rather as the lesser of two evils. Rather, the argument is about who should decide if an abortion is to be carried out.

Those who say that a woman should be free to decide whether or not to have an abortion, generally do so on two grounds:

1. That the foetus is essentially part of a woman's body until it is capable of independent life, and that the potential mother therefore has the moral right to do what she wishes with her potential offspring – simply because, at this stage, the life is seen as potential, rather than actual.

2. That giving birth to children should be seen in terms of the overall situation in which a woman finds herself. She should be free to decide that her own personal development will be stunted by continuing with the pregnancy, or that the financial and social circumstances into which the child would be born would be such that perhaps the whole family might suffer as a result.

In part this argument is utilitarian – weighing the loss of the potential life now against the benefits to the mother and others. But, as it is presented, it is given added force by the use of 'personal development' as an overall criterion of moral choice.

In fact, the criterion of 'personal development' can be used on both sides. In a traditional, 'natural law' based, anti-abortion argument, the baby has a right to be born, irrespective of whether or not he or she could expect to be able to survive after birth, or live in a way that offers a chance of personal development and fulfilment. But, on the other hand, how is one able to tell what the future will hold for that child? I may decide now that there is no chance of personal fulfilment, but, in doing so, I am making a choice in favour of no life, rather than a life of uncertain quality. Yet many people are born into ideal circumstances, but still end up suffering greatly. Is it not morally right, therefore, to offer every individual a chance of personal development (and for that, he or she needs to be born)?

Often, personal development as a criterion gives way to utilitarianism. Development of the mother and existing family now, as opposed to potential development of this new child (with the consequent anticipated loss of potential for others) is balanced. Every utilitarian argument is based on anticipation of future benefits (or lack of them). The fact that the child in this case has not yet been born does not therefore radically alter the way in which an assessment is made – for the future is always unknown.

Perhaps, if those who justify abortion use an act-utilitarian approach, then the anti-abortionists use a rule-utilitarian approach. To argue that the right to destroy life in one situation threatens life everywhere, is a good example of a rule being followed in order that it may maximise happiness for all.

- Arguments about abortion may therefore involve all the forms of ethical justification so far outlined. 'Natural law' is used to protect the unborn child, 'utilitarianism' in both forms is used to assess the result of the abortion, personal development and the freedom of an individual is often the platform from which the 'right to choose' is presented. There is also the sense of a moral absolute, presented by the anti-abortion argument. Those who feel a categorical imperative against killing, will not accept the possibility of willing that everyone should be free to have an abortion.

- Arguments about abortion also tend to illustrate the different forms of moral language:

  - Some will point to statistics, although, as we saw in Chapter 3, 'is' cannot lead directly to 'ought', and the fact that there are a large number of abortions does not in itself show that it is either right or wrong.

  - Some clearly exhibit emotivist language, both in terms of the freedom of choice, and in terms of the revulsion at the destruction of a tiny human life. The two sides seldom come together, because they are based on deeply held emotional commitments.

  - Most arguments are in a prescriptivist form. They are seldom presented out of academic interest only, but plead a cause.

- The newspaper comment, with which this section opened, pointed out that there is little real dialogue between the two sides in this debate. Perhaps the variety of ethical criteria being used illustrates why this is so. It is important, in entering into such moral debates, to be very careful to think through the basis upon which one is arguing.

THE USE OF FERTILISED EMBRYOS

The techniques for artificial fertilisation and selection of embryos raise many ethical problems – both in terms of whether any manipulation of an embryo is a violation of the human rights of the potential person into which it may grow (given the opportunity), and also in terms of the morality of cloning or discarding embryos, or using them for experiments.

A *situation*:

It was reported in the media in October 1993 that scientists in the USA had developed a technique for cloning newly fertilised embryos. The cells were separated from each other after the first cell division. Each carried the same genetic code. This was done on damaged embryos and for experimental purposes only. This technique therefore gives the possibility of cloning individuals.

- If morality is based on the personal development of individuals, is it morally right to produce a clone?

Those who see the personal development of the individual as a valid platform from which to view moral issues will generally consider two things:

1. The choices made by the individual to determine how his or her life should be lived.

2. The freedom that the individual is given in order to be able to make choices and develop himself or herself.

The additional problem raised by the manipulation of fertilised embryos is that factors that will influence characteristics of a future individual (the genes) are being manipulated. Does this mean that character traits in a resulting individual could be blamed on the scientist who conducted the original cloning. 'It's not my fault: I'm made this way!'

This chapter has concentrated on what I have called the 'personal development platform' – looking at the world and its moral choices primarily from the standpoint of the individual. But, of course, it is equally valid to start from a consideration of the needs of society, or of a religious group, or equally of a global need. No one platform is exclusive to an issue: abortion could be seen in a social context, for example, by examining the lack of effective contraception in some societies, or as an issue in a religious view about the protection of all life, or indeed, one might try to bring global population into the argument.

8

— LAW AND ORDER —

— SOCIETY AND MORAL CHOICE —

Some people might want to argue that there is no such thing as 'society': there are just collections of individuals. You cannot ask 'society' what it thinks, you can only ask particular people. Yet people who live together tend to develop sets of principles, expressed sometimes through laws, to make their common life easier. This means that an individual can take these agreed principles or laws into account when faced with a moral dilemma. These principles and laws can be thought of as conventional morality, as expressing the moral views of society as a whole.

In the 5th century BCE, the Greek Sophist Protagoras argued that moral rules were conventions created by society, rather than absolute truths. He believed that they were necessary in order for society to function, but they could be challenged and changed.

However, both Plato and Aristotle wanted to get beyond this idea of conventional morality, to show a link between virtue and happiness. This was in order to get a more objective basis for moral rules – showing them to be in accord with nature. We have already seen the way in which Aristotle's views on this formed the basis of the 'natural law' argument.

In Plato's *Republic*, there is a debate about the function of rules within society. As we saw earlier (when considering freedom),

Thrasymachus argues that conventional justice promotes the interests of the rulers (Marx was not the first to examine society in terms of the struggle between rulers and ruled!), and that the only reasonable basis for ethics is self-interest. Glaucon, in reply, points out that, if everyone acts from selfish motives, then all will end up suffering in some way, exploited by others. The conventional rules, imposed by society, are therefore a way of protecting everyone from the basic selfish desires of everyone else.

Plato wants to take the debate further, and presents the idea that all elements in society (like parts of a human body) need to work together for the general health of the whole. He takes the view that justice offers the happiest life, since it is the expression of health. Injustice is a sickness, from which all are led to suffer. Controlled by reason, Plato considered that happiness lay in achieving a harmony within one's life.

Of course, not everyone is willing or able to think rationally about the moral and social implications of every action. Plato considered (in *The Republic*, Book 11) that society should therefore be ruled by philosophers (since they are able to look at the needs of society as a whole in an unbiased way), and that ordinary people should be required to obey the laws that they devise. But are philosophers really quite as objective and rational as that? Do they not have presuppositions and values of their own to impose?

Both Plato and Aristotle could be said to base their ethics upon reason - as the basis for happiness and the working together of all parts of a society. But one should beware of assuming that they were therefore free from the prejudices of their day. For example, Aristotle (in *Politics*, Book 1, Chapter 5) is quite prepared to say that the proper function of slaves is to obey their masters, and that women should naturally obey men. These are huge social presuppositions that slip into the rational arguments and illustrate the way in which all philosophy (and therefore all ethics) takes place within a particular society, and reflects its values.

We cannot get value-free ethics – for in a value-free situation, most ethical debate would be meaningless. It could be argued that ethics is based on experience and reason, but these alone do not provide the stimulus for the questioning of morality. Computers can handle experience quite effectively, and are also efficient at the application of logic. A computer cannot be moral or immoral, however, because it lacks an inherent set of values with which to assess its choices.

This brief look at early debates on social ethics illustrates three points:

1. Society imposes laws, and encourages moral principles, in order to maintain social cohesion, and minimise damage that would be done by the exercise of unbridled individual desires.

2. Any moral or legal system will therefore be the result of a negotiation between the needs of society as a whole and the freedom of the individual.

3. Rational arguments about the needs of individuals or of society spring from (but may well hide) value judgements and presuppositions.

When we look at moral issues concerned with law and order, and the punishments that society imposes on those who break laws, we need to keep in mind three questions:

- Does society need this particular law for its own well-being?

- Has this law achieved a suitable balance between any conflicting needs of the individual and society?

- Upon what values is it based, and are these values widely accepted within society?

─────── IN WHOSE INTEREST? ───────

In Plato's *Republic*, Thrasymachus argues that justice is the interest of the stronger. A ruler controls his or her subjects, simply because he or she has the authority, backed up by power, to impose chosen laws. Justice therefore depends on the form of government you have. An absolute monarchy will be different from a democracy in the way that its laws are framed and applied.

In modern times, Thrasymachus' views have been reinforced by the Marxist critique of society, in which society progresses by way of conflict between classes. For Marx, the ideal is a classless society in which such struggles are overcome - and in which no one group is therefore able to impose its will on others. His assumption is that, in such a society, the free development of each individual depends upon, and enhances, the development of society as a whole.

But how, in a society of many different people and interests, are you to find a common basis for social ethics? Each person and each group will have particular goals and aspirations. In Plato's *Theaetetus* he ascribed to the Sophist Protagoras the idea that the wind feels cool to one person, but warm to another – and in the same way values depend upon the society within which they are encountered. If there is no general set of values, independent of the form of society in which they are found, how do we assess or criticise any existing legal or social situation?

We therefore need to ask two basic questions:

- Does this imply that there can be no objective standards in law and social morals?

- Is any political system as 'good' as any other? If not, by what criterion can you decide which is better?

—— IS EQUALITY POSSIBLE? ——

In his *Enquiry*, Hume argues that it is impossible to achieve a justice based on what people deserve, simply because people will never be able to agree about what each deserves. But he also felt that it was not practically possible to seek a justice of equality. He sought to protect the property of each person, even though people were unequal in what they owned. He does not say that it would be *wrong* for people to have equal shares, but that it is impractical to expect that such equality could be enforced. The reason he gives is that people are by nature unequal in their abilities, and some will therefore prosper more than others. Whereas an individual act of redistribution might be beneficial (e.g. stealing something that a rich person will not miss, to benefit someone who is poor), the application of that principle to the whole of society would not be practical, and would have harmful consequences.

In this, Hume uses a 'rule utilitarian' argument (see Chapter 5). In the example given above, the point to consider is not 'Will I actually benefit someone by breaking the law of theft in this particular case?' but 'What will be the result of everyone breaking the law of theft in this way?'.

SOCIAL RULES

Laws are created artificially. They are devised by legislators (with or without the consent of the people) and imposed on society. The way in which laws are applied, and the punishments that are appropriate for those who break them may be established by actual cases as they are brought to court.

Some social rules do not have the force of law, but may be established over a period of time by custom. But these too are artificial, and may vary from one society to another.

Some philosophers have put forward ethical theories based on a 'social contract'. This means that an agreement is made between people that they will abide by certain rules, and limit what they are able to do, in order to benefit society, and in order to allow everyone some measure of freedom and security.

HOBBES (1588-1679)

Hobbes argued for a contract to be made between people and their ruler. In such a contract, the ruler should agree to protect the natural rights of the people, to act as an arbiter in any disputes between them, and to make laws in order to establish these things. In return, all who live in the area of the ruler's jurisdiction agree to accept the authority of that ruler, and of such governments and laws as are established. He thought that, if the ruler did not have absolute power, there was a danger of social disintegration – something all too obvious in 17th century England. He therefore placed the ruler above the law.

- For Hobbes, someone taking a minority view, or refusing to agree to any social contract, could not 'opt out' of this arrangement. Simply by living in the geographical area, a person became bound to accept the contract.

LOCKE (1632-1704)

Locke too had a different view. In *The Second Treatise on Civil Government* he argued that people are required to surrender some of their individual rights to the community, but that nobody (and therefore no ruler) should be above the law. Authority should reside in the institutions of state, and these are chosen by the majority of the people. Individuals are given rights – free speech, freedom to worship, freedom to hold property – and it is the duty of government to uphold these rights.

The general principles of individual rights, coupled with democratically supported responsible government, set out by Locke, underlies modern democratic systems. Locke was anti-monarchist, against any one person having absolute power.

ROUSSEAU (1712-1778)

These ideas put forward by Locke are found also in Rousseau. Social contract forms the basis of individual liberty, and in a democracy, people and rulers have the same interests – they work together for mutual benefit. He was therefore against the divine right of Kings, and his ideas influenced the French revolution, which he did not live to see.

He argued that primitive people have two basic emotions; (1) self-preservation and (2) repugnance at the sufferings of others (sympathy). These appear to form quite a reasonable basis for co-operative living. He felt that civilisation, and the rules that go with it, tend to corrupt people (e.g. by imposing ideas of private property, thereby creating inequality and consequent resentment) which destroyed the simplicity and co-operative possibilities of the primitive state.

He argued that under a social contract, imposed by 'the general will' people would agree to give up some of their natural liberty in order to establish 'civil liberty'. In this way, an individual subsumes his or her will to that of the community as a whole.

THOMAS PAINE (1737-1809)

He developed a similar view of the social contract. He argued that an individual should be given liberty, and allowed to do anything (including the right to pursue his or own happiness) as long as no harm is done to others in the process.

Paine's views lies behind the American Declaration of Independence, which allows to each person life, liberty and the pursuit of happiness as a fundamental right.

J S MILL (1806-1873)

Mill highlights one particular feature of the 'social contract'. In *On Liberty*, he is concerned that under a social contract individuals and minority groups might suffer by being made to conform to the wishes of the majority. His answer to this is that a majority should only interfere with a minority, if that minority is doing something that is directly harmful to the interests of the majority.

Therefore, free speech should be allowed, even if the person speaking is thought to be clearly wrong or misguided. He considered that this was less dangerous than allowing an authority to decide what could or could not be said, which would result in a loss of liberty for all.

JOHN RAWLS (1921-)

A modern version of the social contract theory is found in the work of Rawls. In an article entitled 'Justice as Fairness' (1957) and in his major book *A Theory of Justice* (1972) Rawls introduced the idea of 'fairness' into social morality.

He imagined a situation in which a number of people gather together to decide the rules under which they are to live. But they are enabled (by some curious form of amnesia) to forget who they are. They do not know their age, their colour, their wealth, their social position. They decide what they want from society, therefore, without any reference to any special interest group that they might otherwise represent.

He presents two principles upon which justice should be based: (1) that each person has an equal right to the maximum amount of liberty that is compatible with allowing liberty for all and (2) inequalities are only allowed, if there is reason to think that such inequalities will benefit the least well-off in society.

He introduced what he called 'the principle of priority' by which liberties come first, and social equality second. You should not therefore surrender your liberties, even if, by doing so, you could argue that the least well-off in society would benefit.

Rawls thought that people would choose to help the poorest in society because – not knowing whether they themselves were poor or rich when they met together to decide their rules – they would play safe, in case they found that in reality they were in that poorest category.

Notice in these social contract arguments that there is a balance between the rights of an individual and the needs of society. Also, for the democratic and liberal approaches to social morality, it is the individual that takes priority – both by being given rights, and by being allowed a say in the process of government. Any utilitarian argument is therefore tempered by the sense that there are rights to which every individual has a just claim.

A situation:

The public provision of health care would seem to be based on a social contract –people pay money, and the government uses it to provide a service – and also, since it is available to all, it should reflect a fundamental equality of rights. But life is never that easy:

'Doctors clash over smokers' right to life-saving surgery'

'Doctors who deny their patients potentially life-saving operations because they refuse to give up smoking were condemned by the British Cardiac Society, but defended by the British Medical Association...

'The split in medical opinion follows the case of a Manchester man who was refused immediate treatment until he gave up smoking, but who died from a heart attack before he could have tests for a heart bypass operation.'

The argument in favour of offering surgery on the same basis as for non-smokers, is that it is wrong to deny treatment to any group of people, even if they have an added (and voluntary) risk factor. Other people are treated for self-inflicted injuries – hospitals do not require that sportspeople give up their sport before they treat their injuries. Why should smokers be refused treatment on that basis?

Against giving treatment was the medical fact that such surgery was not likely to add to the life expectancy of the patient if he or she continued to smoke.

- The first is based on the idea of fairness within a social contract. The latter is utilitarian – greatest good can be done by allocating treatment where there is likelihood of real benefits.

- Would the force of the argument be different if smoking were illegal?

- The Health Service depends on public funds, and therefore on taxes. Smokers pay tax on their cigarettes. Could it not be argued that, by smoking, they are contributing something extra which should be allocated to helping any resulting disease?

CRIME AND PUNISHMENT

There are, in general, five reasons when society may impose a punishment on those who break the law. They are:

1. To protect society from those who have committed crimes, in order to stop them repeating their offences.

2. To deter others from breaking the law.

3. To reform the criminal.

4. As retribution for the wrong that has been done (i.e. that the person deserves punishment for what he or she has done).

5. To vindicate the law (i.e. without punishments, people will stop respecting the law, and the result will be anarchy).

- Of these, numbers 1, 2, 3 and 5 can be justified on utilitarian grounds. They see punishment as a means of minimising suffering and protecting society. The punishment imposed on one person allows many others to live unmolested.

- Number 4 tends to be defended on the basis of what might be called 'natural justice'. In a natural state, people might be expected to take revenge if they are wronged. Unlimited revenge leads to anarchy. Therefore society limits and regularises what is appropriate by way of punishment.

Just as Kant pointed to a sense of 'ought', that does not depend upon results, so there is a sense that justice requires punishment, irrespective of whether or not anything positive by way of reform or restitution can be achieved by it.

An example:

The British Government 1990 White Paper Crime, Justice and Protecting the Public commented on prisons thus:

'Prison is a society which requires virtually no sense of personal responsibility. The opportunity to learn from other criminals is pervasive. Imprisonment has to be justified in terms of public protection, denunciation or retribution. Otherwise it can be a very expensive way of making bad people worse.'

· If, as this suggests, criminals learn from one another while in prison, can prison be justified on a utilitarian basis? (Except, that is, for those who will spend the rest of their lives in prison.)

· The white paper went on to argue that those who were not violent should, wherever possible, be punished without going to prison.

Points for reflection:

In August 1993, following the leaking of a memorandum about standards of comfort in prisons, there was considerable debate

---

about how prisoners should be treated, and how effective different prison regimes were in preventing prisoners from re-offending. Here are a selection of comments:

> 'What the public expects from the prison system is that it will be frightening enough for potential offenders to deter them from crime.'
>
> [Chairman: Commons Home Affairs Select Committee]

So much for deterrence, but do severe prison regimes actually reform prisoners? This comment is from the director of the Prison Reform Trust:

> 'Candidly, there isn't hard and fast proof one way or the other, but we do know there is a strong relationship between the kind of employment and housing ex-prisoners obtain and whether people re-offend. Common sense tells you that if people feel they are being given opportunities to prepare for that, then that will produce a better result than if they are treated harshly and simply emerge full of resentment and anger.'

And a prison governor commented:

> 'We have to ask: will treating them in a beastly way make them better citizens when they return to ordinary life? I don't think that there is any evidence that if you treat people in a capricious, punitive and uncaring manner they turn out any better than if you treat them with care, consideration and support. It seems clear that the way people are treated affects the way they behave.'

Adding that loss of liberty was punishment in itself

> 'Going to see your kids on sports day, going out for a meal or down the pub, seeing a football match, having a sex life, going on holiday – they have been deprived of all that already. It's a pretty sterile life they lead.'

With these comments, there is need to balance the need to reform with the natural sense that punishment should be unpleasant if it is to deter. Is it possible to run a prison service in which these two goals of punishment are equally balanced? Is it not inevitable that one will always take priority over the other in any one institution?

Various crimes require various forms of punishment – depending on their severity, on the danger posed to society by the person committing the crime, and on the practical implication of the punishment, in terms of whether or not it can reform the criminal, and whether it is necessary to deter others, or to vindicate the law. In terms of the moral issues involved, one form of punishment deserves some special attention:

——— CAPITAL PUNISHMENT ———

As with other life and death issues, there are three main lines of approach here.

1. One is to affirm that there is an absolute right to life, and that nothing can justify taking the life of another human being (this, we have seen, underlies much opposition to both abortion and euthanasia).

2. Another is to take a utilitarian approach – balancing the loss of life against the cost to society of keeping a person in prison for life, or the potential suffering that could result if that person is released from prison and offends again.

3. There is also the need to deter others from committing murder or other serious crimes.

Since the first of these is based either on an absolute moral conviction – either of the 'natural law' or the 'categorical imperative' variety – it is not swayed by the nature of the crime, nor the needs of society. If human life is paramount, then other forms of punishment and protection of society are necessary.

The second and third are made more difficult by the great variety of serious crimes. In the case of murder, many are committed in the course of arguments between close relatives, others take place in the course of robbery or drug dealing, still others are politically motivated, as when a terrorist plants a bomb, or carries out a shooting.

It is difficult to balance the effect of a custodial sentence or capital punishment on either of these – a political murderer may well be prepared to face capital punishment for the sake of martyrdom. On the other hand, a domestic murder may lead to profound remorse, and it is highly unlikely that the person involved would offend again.

In Texas, there are three 'Special Issues' that have to be unanimously agreed by the jury in order to sentence a person to death:

1. that the person deliberately sought the death of his or her victim,

2. that the person would probably commit acts of criminal violence in the future, posing a continuing threat to society,

3. that the murder was not the result of provocation by the victim.

Of these three, the most difficult to decide on ethically is the second. It implies that a person can be punished for a crime that he or she has not yet committed, but might reasonably be expected to commit in the future, if allowed to live.

In considering the utilitarian and deterrence arguments, two things need to be kept in mind. The first is that, from the operation of capital punishment in the United States, it may eventually cost up to six times as much to execute a prisoner as to keep him in prison for life. The reason for this is that execution only takes place after a lengthy series of appeals, which may last many years, and are very expensive. The second point is that, although it is reasonable to assume that the existence of capital punishment should be a deterrent, there is no firm evidence that it actually works as such. Countries with capital punishment do not automatically enjoy a lower incidence of murder.

A further moral point for consideration is whether or not a prisoner should be allowed to choose to be executed, if it is genuinely his or her wish, rather than be kept alive in prison for life. In this case, the utilitarian or deterrence arguments are less relevant. The issue becomes that of the 'right to die', and therefore of the absolute autonomy of the individual.

—— IN SELF DEFENCE? ——

The law does not consider whether something is morally right, but whether or not it is legal. Nevertheless, in looking at evidence in court, a judge and jury have to decide both what actually happened, and whether the person accused actually intended to commit the crime for which he or she is accused. In this, the intention to do something illegal is crucial. This is particularly well illustrated in cases of murder. If the accused killed deliberately, then it is murder. If the killing was done while the person was deranged, or provoked to a point at which he or she lost control, then a charge of manslaughter is considered. If the killing is done in genuine self-defence, then the killing is not a crime. The courts must therefore ascertain a person's intention, as well as his or her actions.

A situation:

In July 1993 a case was brought to trial at the Old Bailey, London, of a teenager who admitted stabbing a man with a knife. The victim had pursued the teenager, who had been slashing car tyres. The teenager had a Swiss army blade, but the man was carrying a hammer. There were no witnesses to the stabbing itself. The teenager claimed that he had been terrified, and that he stabbed the man in self defence.

The following points were made by the judge at the trial, during his summing up:

'Self defence is lawful when it is necessary to use force to resist or defend yourself against an attack or threatened attack and when the amount of force used is reasonable.'

(He added that a person did not have to wait to be struck before defending himself or herself.)

He asked the jury to consider:

- whether the defendant was acting in self defence, or was a willing participant in the violence,

- whether it was necessary to resort to the use of the knife,

---

- whether the defendant was using no more force than was reasonably necessary.

Reasonable force depended, he argued, upon the nature of the attack, but that:

> '.. a person defending himself cannot be expected to weigh precisely the exact amount of defensive action that is necessary.
> 'If therefore the defendant did no more than what he instinctively thought was necessary, that is very strong evidence that the amount of force was reasonable and necessary.'

And, since a person is innocent until proven guilty, is was up to the prosecution to prove that the stabbing was not self defence, rather than for the accused to prove that it was.

The teenager was found not guilty of murder.

[Reported in *The Daily Telegraph*, July 15th 1993]

That is the legal situation, but from an ethical point of view there are other points to consider:

• Was the man right to pursue a young person whom he had found committing an act of vandalism, or should he have simply reported it to the police? Should individual citizens seek to take the law into their own hand and apprehend culprits?

• Do you have a responsibility to take action if you see a crime being committed? If not, are you (by your inaction) condoning that particular crime?

• Are you therefore morally responsible not just for what you do, but for what you know is being done? (If it lies within your power to do something to stop it.)

A *further example:*

Two men from a Norfolk village (referred to in newspaper reports as 'village vigilantes') lay in wait for a local teenager, whom they suspected of stealing. They forced him into a van, tied his hands and threatened him with violence. They freed him, unharmed, twenty minutes later.

> *They were sentenced to five years in jail for kidnapping. On appeal, their sentences were cut to six months, much to the satisfaction of a large number of villagers, who had campaigned on their behalf.*
>
> - The argument against the vigilantes was that you cannot uphold the law by breaking it —which they did by kidnapping the youth. That argument is independent of the issue of whether the youth was or was not actually guilty of any offences.
>
> - Notice that with the earlier situation, the intention was all important. To commit murder you have to intend to kill. Here, however, the intention is overruled by the action. It is not enough to say that the men 'intended' simply to warn the youth about what would happen if he stole things – since they actually carried out (and pleaded guilty to) the crime of kidnapping.

The second case raises an important issue of social morality. There are things that one person can do but another cannot. A surgeon can cut a person open with a knife: his social function makes that quite reasonable. If I were to walk into a hospital wearing a white coat and brandishing a scalpel, I would not be morally justified in going to work in the operating theatre!

On this basis, it is quite lawful for a policeman to arrest a suspect, to bind his hands in handcuffs, and to take him to a police station. There he may be spoken to very sternly, threatened with legal action if he is apprehended committing a crime, and then (following a formal caution, if he has been caught actually committing a minor offence) released.

The problem with the vigilantes is that they were taking on themselves a role for which society has agreed that only certain people are to perform.

Of course, if the two vigilantes had caught the youth in the act of committing a crime, and had forcibly taken him to a police station (provided that no unreasonable force was used), then they would have been carrying out a citizen's arrest, which is legal.

—— CIVIL DISOBEDIENCE ——

Do you have an absolute duty to obey the law of the land? Are there occasions when it would be right to break the law?

You could argue, for example, that if a law goes against fundamental human rights, then the law is in the wrong and should be opposed. Remember that laws are artificial things, devised and imposed. Even though, according to the theory of social contract, they may have been established by the agreement of a majority of people, that does not mean that they are absolute – they are not created by logical necessity, and do not apply to all people at all times.

Those who contemplate civil disobedience might want to take the following into consideration:

- Is the law the product of a democratic process? If there are no democratic controls on the law, then you could argue (on utilitarian grounds) that it is right to oppose the law for the benefit of the greater number of people. This would be the case if there was a law that was imposed on people, but benefited only the ruler or a small elite, rather than the people as a whole. On the other hand, if the law is established within a democracy, then you cannot argue that opposing it will be in the interests of a majority unless you believe that the majority were duped by the rulers or legislators. 'We didn't realise, when we elected this government, that this would be the result' would be an argument of this sort.

- Is there any other way in which you can pursue the cause that you are supporting? For example, can the law be changed? If so, by whom? Can you influence those who can do so?

- Is there a categorial imperative – a sense of moral obligation that is absolute, and that stands in contrast to the law in question. In this case, you may feel that you are justified in challenging or breaking the law. Although, of course, you may need to be prepared to take the consequences in terms of any punishments that society may impose on you.

A *situation:*

In 1990, there were demonstrations in Britain against the Community Charge (commonly known as the 'Poll Tax') a form of taxation which many felt was unfair. A large number of people refused to pay the tax - an act of civil disobedience.

Writing in the The Independent *under the headline 'When civil disobedience is right', Tony Benn, a Member of Parliament said:*

> 'The idea that "conscience is above the law" is deeply entrenched in our collective sub-conscious and even a decade in which the Dow Jones Industrial Average has been worshipped in preference to the Ten Commandments has absolutely failed to obliterate an old conviction that what is morally wrong can never be politically right.
>
> 'It is time that we all understood exactly how civil disobedience operates to achieve results in a nation that enjoys ballot box democracy, for in such circumstances public opinion has often forced a change through Parliament by bringing pressure to bear upon the elected government.'
>
> [From an article in *The Independent*, March 28th 1993]

This raises an important issue for the relationship between the law and morality. What Tony Benn is saying is that, when the cause is morally right, civil disobedience is a valid way to exert political pressure and therefore change the law.

Other points to consider:

- Non payment of a tax is an act of direct non-violent civil disobedience. But what of a violent demonstration (there were violent demonstrations against the poll tax the following month)? If violence is a breakdown of law and order, can it ever be a valid way of promoting changes to the law?

- Perhaps, in assessing the place of such violence, one might test it in the same way that the person who claims to have killed in self-defence can defend himself. Is the violence 'necessary'? Is it in proportion to the threat?

REVOLUTIONARY CHANGE

Although there are acts of civil disobedience from time to time, it is more usual for laws to change because the democratic process that framed them is such that it allows for such change through its normal legislative procedures. Changes like this come because of practical or scientific advances (e.g. the time limit on termination of pregnancy was lowered in Britain in 1990 because scientific advances were allowing the survival of foetuses at an earlier stage), or because the attitudes of society change (e.g. the legalising of homosexual acts in private between consenting adults).

- If laws can be changed peacefully, then – on the basis of utilitarianism, or social contract, it would be right to avoid any violence or revolution.

- If the law cannot be changed peacefully, then (on a utilitarian basis) an assessment should be made about whether the cost of that change, in terms of suffering or loss of life, is worth the benefits to be gained through the revolutionary change.

- Violence could be justified on a utilitarian basis if it were to be shown that it is simply a defence against an already existing violence. For example, it might be argued that a repressive regime imposed such financial hardship on its people that it amounts to 'economic violence'. In this case, some people might argue that it could legitimately be opposed by physical violence.

ASSESSING RESULTS

Changes in society come about for a variety of reasons; some political, some economic, some because of a gradual change in attitudes and values. It is sometimes difficult to assess exactly how much change has been brought about by exactly which political actions. There could be a violent demonstration against a law, but at the same time there could be a sense of general dissatisfaction with it, and a recognition on the part of a democratic government that it will not be re-elected if it does not change the law. Are those who took part in the violent demonstration therefore entitled to claim that their violence was justified, since their chosen end has actually come about. Might it not have happened anyway?

WHO TAKES RESPONSIBILITY?

When people are involved in civil disobedience, or in the violent overthrow of a government, they tend to become bolder as they act together in a group. In the course of a demonstration, for example, there might be a great deal of damage done, looting of shops etc. The general atmosphere of violence and change appears to sanction the sort of actions which individuals might not contemplate in more peaceful times.

- Does this loss of social restraint justify individual acts of violence against people or property?

> ***For reflection:***
>
> In time of war, killing is sanctioned – and what would have been murder in peacetime becomes part of the duty of members of the armed forces. This distinction becomes blurred for people who, attempting to change the political situation by the use of violence, see themselves as taking part in a military campaign. For example, the IRA may refer to its members in Northern Ireland or mainland Britain, as belonging to 'active service units' – which implies a military context in which soldiers are given orders, and are expected to kill the 'enemy'. Yet, since no war has been declared, the same activities are regarded by those outside the organisation as straightforward cases of murder.

—— IF NIETZSCHE WERE A CIVIL —— SERVANT...

Civil servants generally operate along carefully controlled and monitored lines.

First of all they gather data. They produce reports, with statistical evidence set out. To do this they gather together advisers, experts in particular fields. They are required to be well informed.

Based on that information, they set about implementing the will of their political masters. In doing this, they are governed by two things – the laws of the land, and the goals that politicians have set. What they do may be monitored through their own checking process within the civil service, and also through select committees which can require them to explain their actions.

A good civil servant is meant to have no political views. His or her task is simply to act on the guidelines given, within the constraints of budgets, national and international law. The criterion upon which a civil servant is often judged is not whether the decisions implemented were right or wrong – that is something for politicians to sort out – but whether he or she was effective in putting them into practice.

Civil servants, like chess players, work creatively within carefully controlled and defined structures. They are answerable only for decisions made within a very specific brief. Ultimately, they have no 'I' that operates in choosing what to do. They use personal judgement, of course (which is why they cannot be replaced by computers), but their judgements are based on values that are given to them, not generated by them.

That does not mean that civil servants are without power; but their power lies in their ability to manipulate rules and values to their own advantage.

Contrast the civil servant with the campaigner. A campaigner is someone who takes up an issue, decides on a particular point of view, and argues it with moral conviction. Campaigners lobby politicians – they present one side of an argument, the side about which they feel strongly. They tend to be visionary, to think long-term, to be idealist in their aspirations. They are frustrated by bureaucracy, by restrictive legislation. They wish to change laws by changing the values and priorities upon which those laws are based.

Between the civil servant and the campaigner lies the politician. Some might be presented as genuine transmitters of the values and aspirations of those they represent, seeking to frame laws that will benefit their constituents. Others might be presented as followers of Machiavelli, seeking their own power, and ruthless to maintain their establishment.

In either case, in order to survive, a politician has to take a line that is half-way between the campaigner and the civil servant. He or she has to explore situations and values, and use them as the basis of legislation.

One could imagine a television sitcom involving a civil servant and politician and a campaigner – in a caricature, their styles of speech, dress and lifestyle would be quite different from one another.

Alongside the political and civil establishment is the judiciary. Judges, magistrates and lawyers seek to implement law, but they do so with a degree of flexibility that allows the particular situation to influence the application of the general rule. Moral questions are sometimes raised when it is considered that a particular legal decision strays too far from the general rule. For example, when a person found guilty of rape is given a very light sentence, or someone is fined heavily for dropping litter. The judge is required to be an expert in law, a balanced assessor of what is appropriate in terms of punishment, and also a subtle inquisitor of human nature, and of the way in which values and laws impinge on each individual.

These characters have been introduced (albeit in the form of caricature) to illustrate different positions that may be taken in terms of the ethics of law and society. All are needed in society. Without the campaigner, there is no direct application of values to practical issues. Without the politician there is no way of formulating laws for the common good based on those values. Without the civil servant, there is no application of laws to specific situations. Without the judge there is no application of law to individual situations in a way which allows justice to operate on an individual level.

Some thinkers might easily be typecast as one or other of these characters. Machiavelli, for example, would clearly do rather better as a politician than as a judge or campaigner! He might also do well as a civil servant – but he would have to be very skilled in achieving his goals without appearing to break too many of the rules under which he would be required to operate.

But what about Nietzsche? Is it possible to act as a civil servant if one's ultimate criterion of right and wrong is defined in terms of the ability of individuals to overcome themselves and develop something higher. Is it possible to promote personal evolution at the same time as maintaining social cohesion?

Nietzsche, as was pointed out in the last chapter, was a shrewd observer of the loss of faith in the 19th century, and he was not afraid to explore the consequences that this might have for morality, and for human values in general. His 'will to power', like Hobbes' assertion that everything one does has one's own 'good' as an aim, is an observation of what, in fact, appears to take place as people make choices.

It is grossly unfair to see Nietzsche only from the perspective of those who later took some of his ideas (particularly that of the 'Superman') as the basis for racist elitism. The Nazi party in Germany, seeking to promote the idea of a superior Aryan race, exhibited a ruthless disregard of human life in the extermination of Jews, of gypsies, of the mentally ill. Nietzsche, by contrast, when he (in the person of Zarathustra) comes down the mountain to proclaim the 'Superman', he declares that he comes to bring humankind a gift, and when the tightrope walker falls to the earth, overtaken by the buffoon who has leaped over him, Zarathustra comforts the dying man and takes him for burial. Man - as he crossed the rope stretched between ape and superman - will fall, but will also deserve decent burial.

Yet this should not blind us to the central challenge of Nietzsche - in the absence of 'God' (in the form of a set of structures and values in the world), by what criterion – other than the development of that which is 'beyond' each individual in terms of personal development – can one judge what is right?

- Is society there fundamentally as the environment in which each individual can grow to his or her full potential? Or is the individual simply one part of a social pattern, defined and valued within it?

Both perspectives – the personal and the social – are needed. Neither makes sense without the other. But in moral debate there is a constant process of balancing the two: too far one way and the result is anarchy and chaos, too far the other and there is authoritarian rule and loss of personal freedom.

In an ideal ethical system (and an ideal world within which to operate it) every social contract would allow the personal development of each individual. Equally, personal development would enhance the relationships of which society is made up. If (like Rawls) we could see the world from a completely selfless point of view, then the ideal system might be devised. Unfortunately, no such global amnesia exists, and self-interest remains a powerful feature in human choice.

9

A GLOBAL PERSPECTIVE

A global perspective may involve two things:

- issues that concern the international community.

- issues that concern the relationship between the human species and its environment, including the other species with which it shares the planet.

INTERNATIONAL ETHICS

In his book, *The Moral Philosophers,* Richard Norman sets out the case for a naturalistic approach to ethics. He makes the important point that such ethics must take into account both the needs of the individual, and also his or her social relationships. Whether through Marx (in the idea of the need to overcome alienation in work) or Freud (in the fundamental need for sexual fulfilment), or the whole spectrum of philosophers from Plato and Aristotle onwards, he points out that ethics needs to be rooted also in social and political philosophy – for an account of how a moral life brings satisfaction is linked (and has been since the Greeks tended to exclude slaves and women from the sphere of free moral thoughts) to the prevailing social ethos.

In other words, social ethics needs to be rooted in a common understanding of society and shared values.

How then do we understand international ethics? There is no single global ideology. There is no single global religion. There is no single global political system. The only areas in which there seems to be a global web of influence are that of money (where competition in international markets has international consequences) and ecology (where destruction of the environment in one place may have effects that are felt globally), both of which involve competition rather than agreement.

And yet there has been an explosion of information from all parts of the globe. If there is famine, war, or natural disaster, we see it on our television screens. Such information, in the absence of effective international co-operation, leads to frustration, and the moral determination that 'something must be done'.

THE INTERNATIONAL COMMUNITY

There are two ways of approaching the ethical guidelines for international relationships:

1. Work on the basis of the basic human rights that should be allowed to every human being, irrespective of the sort of political, social or religious community in which he or she lives.

   Examples of this are the United Nations Universal Declaration on Human Rights, and also the Geneva Convention, which deals with the conduct of war and the treatment of prisoners. Such an approach also recognises the integrity and national sovereignty of individual countries. For this reason the United Nations will only operate within a country if it is invited to do so by those whom it recognises as the legal government.

   A major problem with this approach is that it is difficult to enforce these standards. Without the equivalent of an international police force, capable of requiring individual nations to comply, all the international community can do is to try to exert political or economic pressure in the hope that an individual country may eventually come to the conclusion that it is in its own best interests to comply with the will of the majority. Where one nation invades another, the United

Nations may be involved in an attempt at peacekeeping, but has no authority to threaten or carry out an invasion of the aggressor nation in order to stop that aggression.

2. Take a utilitarian approach. This could seek to take into account the preferences of the maximum number of people. But utilitarianism comes up against two major problems when applied to these global issues:

(a) A person may have conflicting loyalties. I may think of myself as a citizen of a particular country, or of a wider grouping of nations. But I may first of all think of myself as coming from a particular county, or even village. In times of civil war, local loyalties conflict with national ones.

An Example:

During the war in Bosnia, people of different ethnic groups, who had previously lived together peacefully as part of a village community, were suddenly thrust apart, and regarded one another as enemies, each supporting a national rather than a local identity.

- Does being a Serb or a Croat count for more than being a member of a particular village?

- It is right to take action against former neighbours who are from a different ethnic or national group, just because the majority of members of your own group demand that you do so?

- Is it right to take action just because a majority of people from my particular ethnic group would prefer me to do so?

Thus it is very difficult to find a consensus as to what most people would prefer, or what could actually be expected to bring the greatest happiness to the greatest number of people.

(b) Without any international standards with regard to what people consider the necessities of life, it is difficult to know how best to share out the world's resources. What might be regarded as living on the poverty line in Northern Europe, might seem like luxury for someone from the more impoverished nations of Africa, for example.

Nevertheless, most issues of international aid, or warfare, imply a combination of both ethical processes. There is talk of human rights and responsibilities, but there is also the utilitarian redistribution of wealth.

If the international community does not invade the national sovereignty of the aggressor state, it limits its operation to attempts at peacekeeping, monitoring human rights, exerting external political pressure and delivering humanitarian aid, its perception of what is possible is constantly changing with the fortunes of the war.

In the case of Bosnia during the course of 1993, what was regarded as quite unacceptable early in the year became a basis for negotiation later on, as military advances claimed more ground. United Nations troops were required to watch as the war moves across the face of what was once a sovereign state, monitoring human rights, protesting at abuses, and seeking to explore a peaceful solution acceptable to all sides. The United Nations agreed, however, that its forces could take direct military action, if necessary.

The whole dilemma of the ethics of international relations is that there are few means of enforcing the decisions taken. There is a gap between what may be perceived as right, and what is possible. Whether it is in the field of national sovereignty, or of destruction of the environment, the only available means of persuasion are argument, economic and political pressure, and exclusion from international bodies – and for some nations, their own internal perceptions and aspirations take priority over those of the international community.

International pressure is brought to bear, however, by the threat to withhold the normal process of international trade, in the form of sanctions, or the cutting of international political or financial ties. The problem is that such pressure works long-term, whereas the issue it is meant to address is immediate.

For reflection:

Machiavelli recommended that, if a ruler had to administer punishment, he should do it quickly and efficiently. This would produce least resentment. But sanctions – as a means of enforcing international agreements – produce their results only slowly, and maximise resentment. They may effect all those who live in a country, not just its rulers, and may produce a sense of national solidarity. On the other hand, sanctions do not generally involve loss of life.

There seems to be no way in which an international moral code could be translated into enforceable laws without loss of the principle of national sovereignty. The nearest that the United Nations would appear to come to such a situation is, for example, in the terms imposed on Iraq after the Gulf War. This includes 'no fly' zones over areas of the north and south of the country – seeking to give some protection for the Kurds and the Marsh Arabs respectively. But even so, without military on the ground, it is impossible to prevent persecution of minority groups within a state.

But here there is another dilemma. If you maintain national sovereignty, how do you deal fairly with those groups of people who do not form a nation? An example of this is the Kurds. They are found in Iraq, Iran and Turkey.

For reflection:

- Is it better for a nation to keep its borders open to receive those who are fleeing persecution in other parts of the world, or to close them, in order to preserve the standard of living of its own citizens?

- In a democracy, should people be balloted on whether or not to allow citizens from other countries to receive an entry permit?

- If its own citizens enjoy a far higher standard of living, compared with the refugees, are they morally required to take a small cut in their own standards, in order that their government can offer a considerably improved standard of living to the refugees?

LEAVE IT TO CHARITIES?

Many charities operate internationally. They respond to need and provide a means by which people who feel that they have a moral responsibility to help are able to give practical expression to their moral convictions. But typically, charities depend on:

- political co-operation from the country within which they wish to operate

- a cessation of military action – or at least the agreement of the warring factions that the charities can operate.

So charitable help depends on agreements which concern national sovereignty and the terms and conditions under which wars are fought. When we look at ethics from a global perspective, we therefore have to address these issues – because, however much people wish to respond charitably, the help that can be given is limited, or short term, without political stability and peace.

WHO IS RESPONSIBLE?

Sometimes an individual – perhaps a head of state – is portrayed as being personally responsible for an issue which has international moral repercussions (e.g. Colonel Gadaffy of Libya is sometimes presented as personally responsible for decisions about the support of 'terrorists'; similarly, Saddam Hussein of Iraq was shown very much as a figure upon whom people were invited to focus their moral indignation at the time of the Gulf War).

More often, however, international ethics concerns the relationships between institutions rather than individuals. Institutions are controlled by charters, and are required to operate within legally enforceable rules. It is not therefore immediately obvious who is morally responsible for the actions of an institution.

For reflection:

If you are in charge of an institution, you may act as its figurehead, and thus be seen as an appropriate person to blame if things go wrong. But:

Should a Minister of State be the person to resign if there is a scandal within his Ministry? Is the Chief Executive of a charity responsible for individual decisions taken by his or her staff?

- Are you morally responsible for all those things which are done in your name (or in the name of an institution you represent)?

- If you knew something was wrong, but took no action, you had a moral choice. You are responsible – not for the original wrong, but for your own inaction.

- If you were not told that anything was wrong – can you be blamed for not knowing, and therefore not acting? Surely, your responsibility in this case is to be well informed – and if you have not done everything within reason to find out what is happening, you might be guilty of negligence? But does your negligence mean that you are guilty of whatever has gone wrong?

THE JUST WAR

In the 13th century, Thomas Aquinas argued that three conditions had to be met before a war could be called 'just'.

1. It should be undertaken only by those with proper authority in a nation. Thus, even if it is morally right for a ruler (civil or military), or an elected government, to declare war, it would not be right, in the same circumstances, for a single citizen to take up weapons and attack the enemy.

[This requirement is made far more difficult in the case of civil war. One has to decide who should have the authority to act on behalf of the country as a whole.]

2. There should be good reasons for going to war. For example, it would be justified if it were done in national self-defence.

3. The intention of going to war should be a good one. In other words, you should not declare war just for the sake of killing, but in the hope of establishing peace and justice as a result of it.

And there are two other criteria generally used alongside these first three:

- War should be waged against the military, not against civilians.

- The force used should be in proportion to the ends to be achieved.

An example:

When rivalry between the nuclear superpowers – the United States, and the then Soviet Union – was at its height, there was a principle of nuclear deterrence knows as MAD. This stood for Mutually Assured Destruction. According to this theory, each side held enough weaponry, both in terms of first strike capability, and second strike response, to guarantee that, if attacked, it would be capable of retaliating with such force as to guarantee that any attacking nation would be destroyed.

The nuclear deterrent theory was that while each side was capable of destroying the other, neither would actually use such weapons and peace would thus be maintained.

- This is a moral theory of which Machiavelli would have been proud. It is a 20th century equivalent of his insistence that the threat of force is the best way to maintain security.

- Deterrence theory could be justified by a combination of Machiavellian pragmatism and utilitarianism. On this basis, wars between non-nuclear states could result in loss of life, because such states could attack one another in the hope of genuinely making some sort of political gain. On the other hand, the nuclear superpowers could not attack one another,

---

because each knew that it faced certain destruction if it did so. Thus, on the basis that citizens of neither country would choose to die in a nuclear holocaust - nor would they like to be under non-nuclear threat if they had no means of retaliation – the happiness of the greatest number was maintained by retaining and always threatening to use nuclear weapons.

Now, in terms of the traditional 'just war' terms, there could be no justification for actually waging nuclear war, because:

- It would inevitably lead to considerable civilian loss of life.

- It would not involve force in proportion to its aims. In other words, a just war should use the minimum force necessary to achieve what the war set out to achieve, and that could not happen through a general use of nuclear weapons.

- It could not have as its aim the establishment of peace and justice, if its result was a widespread killing with possible global repercussions for many years to come.

On the other hand, if deterrence works, is that not in itself sufficient justification for its adoption as a military policy?

The earlier arguments about nuclear weapons, based on the MAD theory and visions of global holocaust, have given way to two other difficult moral questions:

1. In a situation where a limited use of nuclear weapons could bring to an end a conventional war, and thereby save a greater number of lives, is it not morally wrong (on utilitarian grounds) to refuse to use it? This, of course, was the sort of reasoning used to justify the first nuclear devices used against Japan – claiming that they shortened the war in the Far East. It became more relevant with the development of tactical and intermediate nuclear weapons, and the theoretical possibility of waging a limited nuclear war, even against a nuclear opponent.

   Some might therefore argue that a limited nuclear exchange would be morally right, on the 'just war' theory – since, although the form of weapon is different, the overall amount of force being used is not increased.

2. In the post-Cold War situation, with a reduction in the stocks of nuclear weapons, the question arises as to whether maintaining any such weapons is justified.

   Some would argue in favour of holding nuclear weapons on grounds of national security, using the deterrence argument, as set out above. Even if Mutually Assured Destruction was not guaranteed, any aggressor would be liable to suffer a limited nuclear retaliation, which would be enough to discourage the aggressor.

In spite of changes in the international balance of power, arms stocks and nuclear technology, there remain some fundamental ethical issues:

* Is it ever morally right to threaten to do something, if actually doing it would be morally wrong?

* Are there forms of weaponry (nuclear, chemical, biological), the impact of which is so horrific that their use can never be justified, even if (using a utilitarian argument) there is reasonable expectation of long-term benefit?

There are a variety of positions that can be taken on the involvement of one nation in the affairs of another, as the following example illustrates:

An example:

In August 1993, while Serb forces ringed the Bosnian capital, Sarajevo, a number of eminent people in Britain were asked their views on whether or not Britain should become involved militarily in an attempt to stop the war. Here are some of the responses:

'I'm very doubtful about it. In circumstances of this kind, the international community has two functions – to provide humanitarian aid, and to sponsor peace talks. To involve our forces as combatants in a Balkan war would be to involve them in consequences the end of which we cannot foresee.'

'We should have taken action much earlier – by not doing so, we have set a very dangerous precedent...'

'I have expressed myself opposed to the involvement of British forces. This is because it doesn't concern us, and there is therefore no justification for committing the forces of the Crown.'

'The danger is that we would get sucked into commitments we can't afford.'

'Serbian aggression cannot be allowed to continue unchecked...'

'I don't agree with the use of armed force. There is no way of knowing what the outcome would be. The only way of resolving the present conflict is through negotiations between the Bosnians and the Serbs. Military measures usually serve to make matters more difficult.'

[Quotes taken from 'Moral conflict or military quagmire', article by Paul Goodman, *The Sunday Telegraph*, August 8th 1993]

Those who get closest to the scenes of fighting without actually being involved include journalists. They are rightly accused sometimes of sensationalism, but equally they are the ones who actually see and report on what, for others at a safe distance, is a matter of detached debate. Here is one such reaction, by Patrick Bishop in July 1993, to the war in Bosnia:

'When I first visited Bosnia a year ago, I remember the shock of seeing a frightened Muslim family, perched on their belongings on a horse-drawn cart, trundling through the streets of Sanski Most after being driven from their village. That this could happen in Europe in 1992 seemed an obscenity. Later such scenes, multiplied a thousandfold, became almost banal.'

In the same article he noted the scale of the suffering, throughout the previous 14 months of war – 140,000 dead (mostly civilians), two million people homeless, destruction and dislocation of whole populations.

He notes the suffering inflicted and received by all sides in the war, but, commenting on the plight of the Muslims in Bosnia, he makes the point that they will have learned two lessons:

1.'.. the need for self-reliance: that no matter how just your cause, neither the media nor anyone else can be depended on to save you. Hours of harrowing television pictures have created a climate of deep sympathy for the victims. But this has not translated into a public movement for intervention. Neither Washington nor any European government has been under significant pressure to become involved in an inevitably bloody peace-enforcement operation.'

2.'.. that without that pressure, and without the perception that some vital interest is threatened, Europe and America will ultimately be prepared to sit back and watch a crime being committed before their eyes.'

And from these he draws a general conclusion that has profound moral implications for the international community:

'The basic message is that the world community will enforce the principle that land should not be acquired by force only where a crucial strategic interest is at stake. It is a signal that will be welcomed by irredentists and aggressive nationalists everywhere.'

[From an article by Patrick Bishop, *The Daily Telegraph*, July 1st 1993]

- If this really is the situation in international affairs, on what basis are nations operating?

- If there is a conflict between a moral obligation to right a perceived injustice and self-interest, is it inevitable that the latter will prevail?

- In international moral issues, should the needs of individual nation states be paramount? If they are, is there any basis upon which one nation will effectively aid another against its own best interests?

A situation:

A few days before the publication of the above article, the United States launched an attack on Baghdad using 23 ship-launched cruise missiles. They destroyed the headquarters of Iraqi intelligence, but three missiles went astray, destroying homes in Baghdad and killing eight civilians. Each missile carried a 1,000 lb high-explosive warhead.

The reason given for the attack was that the US had evidence of a plot to assassinate George Bush, the former President of the United States, during his visit to Kuwait in April of that year. In a statement to an emergency meeting of the United Nations, the US ambassador said that the purpose of the raid was to:

'reduce the Iraqi regime's ability to promote terrorism and deter further aggression against the US ....'

and having given evidence of the planned assassination she said to the UN Security Council

'In our judgment, every member here today would regard an assassination attempt against its former head of state as an attack against itself and would react.'

Other countries, including Britain and France, gave support to the action of the United States.

President Clinton, in a television address to the American people, explaining the raid, described Saddam as 'a tyrant who repeatedly violated the will and conscience of the international community.'

- Was the US justified in carrying out a raid on the basis of a failed assassination attempt?

- Is it right that an attack on a former head of state should be considered an attack upon the state which he headed, and therefore justify an armed retaliation?

- What does the contrast between the actions of the United States in this instance, and the inability of the UN or other powers to take military steps in Bosnia, suggest in terms of the general moral principles in the international sphere?

These questions do not imply criticism of the actions of the United States, but they are relevant in assessing the rights of nations to take direct action against one another. It should be noted, of course, that the dispute between Iraq and the United States stemmed from Iraq's invasion of Kuwait – a country over which it claimed sovereignty – and the war which followed.

In the USA public reaction was favourable:

'By a margin of more than two to one, Americans supported the

notion that the raid was "a good idea because it teaches Saddam Hussein a lesson" over the view that it was a "bad ideas because it risks further bloodshed".'
[From an article by Stephen Robinson, *The Daily Telegraph*, June 30th 1993]

Notice that this reflects an absolutist rather than a utilitarian approach to the idea of punishment – that the punishment should be appied because it is deserved, quite apart from any consideration of its possible consequences.

The contrast between the response to Iraq's action against Kuwait, and the inability to check or oppose the Serb move against Bosnia, gives cause to question again whether any principle other than perceived long-term self-interest operates in the international sphere.

POVERTY AND INTERNATIONAL AID

In his book *Practical Ethics*, Peter Singer argued that, if deliberately allowing people to die is no different (in moral terms) from actually killing them, then we are all guilty of murder, since we allow a situation to continue in which millions of people starve to death. On the other hand, he recognised that cutting one's standard of living to the bare minimum, in order to do all that might be possible to help others to life, would require a 'moral heroism' which is far greater than simply refraining from killing.

A point for reflection:

Imagine a situation where people from various developed and developing countries are sitting in a single room, each in the exact situation which would apply in his or her home territory. In one corner people would be naked and starving, in another they would be well clothed and fed.

In such a situation, it would not be too difficult to imagine sharing both food and clothes. Indeed, it would be very difficult not to do so, since the emotional impact of the proximity of poverty and starvation would be intense.

But the single room situation is an unrealistic abstraction. In practice, it is easy to refrain from sharing necessities because:

• No one individual is to blame.

• Social pressures and expectations are connected with a particular standard of living, to give all that up and accept shared poverty would require great determination. It might also affect others, who would not share your personal commitment to such poverty.

• Although they can be seen on television, for much of the time the starving are out of sight. Although there is intellectual awareness of their plight, there is no immediate emotional pressure to respond, in the way that there might be if they were visible and present.

• When confronted with a particular emotional challenge, practical steps can follow. But in this process, rational commitment takes the place of emotional response, e.g. many people respond emotionally to appeals on the television; some go on to make a practical response, by donating money. A few are moved by this and actually take on a longer term commitment – as when Bob Geldof was moved by reports of the starving in Ethiopia in 1984, and as a result went on to found Band Aid, and the Live Aid concerts, in order to raise money and awareness to benefit those who were starving.

• It is easy to justify inaction, on the (valid) grounds that much poverty is not caused by simple lack of food, but by the political situation. Most areas of starvation are also those hit by military conflict. In the absence of such conflict, it is easier for people to move and get food, or for external agencies to give aid effectively. It is also possible to plan long-term agriculture development if there is peace.

Aid is therefore a complex issue - and it cannot be reduced to the 'single room' situation. Some major ethical issues connected with it are:

• How, on a utilitarian basis, do you determine what is an appropriate level of wealth or poverty? (One person aspires to a level of material support that another might fear, thinking it the most abject poverty.)

- How do you give aid, whilst maintaining the personal integrity and independence of the people who receive that aid. (This is based on the moral principle which sees human autonomy and independence as of primary importance.)

- Can any individual be held morally responsible for a global situation? If not, is there corporate guilt, shared by all people of a particular nation, class, or economic level? (This is a real issue, for there have been riots connected with economic and social groups, e.g. migrant workers.)

- Does the presence of a factor over which I can have no control (e.g. a civil war in a developing country) be justification for taking no action to alleviate a condition which, in theory, I can control, (e.g. giving a donation to an aid agency to help famine relief, even though that agency realises that the underlying cause of the famine requires a political solution).

So far, everything we have been considering has been concerned with the way in which human beings treat one another, but humankind is just one of many species who inhabit this planet, and so it is natural to ask if the sort of moral considerations that have been applied to the treatment of other human beings should be extended to include other species.

This does not imply that animals should behave morally – for without reason, morality makes no sense. A cat, offered the prospect of tormenting and killing a mouse, acts instinctively, but (as we shall consider in a moment) humans can choose how they will behave towards other species.

ANIMAL RIGHTS

Most moral arguments are based on human needs and human happiness. But do we as a species have any moral obligations towards other species? Do animals have rights and, if so, how are those rights assessed?

Let us look at the way in which some ethical arguments might be applied to animals.

FAIRNESS

Ethical theories that are based on the idea of a social contract that is drawn up between people are concerned with the fairness that exists within a relationship. Each party accepts responsibilities and in return receives rights. Can this sort of theory be applied to other species?

A pet is accepted into a human social setting for the benefit of the humans. For example, looking after a pet hamster may be a way of encouraging children to take responsibility generally, as well as giving them pleasure. A dog or cat may be good company, especially for people living on their own. A family pet may be thought to offer something positive to the life and atmosphere of a family home. A relationship develops between the pet animal and the humans, through expressions of affection and shared enjoyments (like dog and owner taking walks together).

In what way does the animal benefit from this arrangement? By being given food and shelter, veterinary care and all else needed to enable it to live out its natural lifespan in a measure of comfort seldom offered in its natural habitat?

If animals are treated cruelly when they are forced to live in the human environment, then it is clear that the humans have not acted fairly in terms of the implied contract between themselves and the animal. If you accept a pet, you have a responsibility to care for it in a way that is appropriate to its needs.

NATURAL LAW

It might be argued that humans have no right to be entering into such implied contracts with animals at all. The Islamic view of life, for example, is that animals should not be kept as pets or put into zoos. It regards this as basically unnatural, and therefore as violating the natural life and instincts of the animal.

In this case, the argument being used is one of 'natural law' – that animals have their natural place within the scheme of things, and should not be treated as pets. Respect for the animal demands that it should be treated as an animal, not as a quasi-human, manicured, clipped and paraded!

On the other hand, animals in the wild feed on one another. Humans are omnivorous, and therefore have a choice – they can either eat other species of animal or remain vegetarian. A natural law argument might well accept that there is a place for the eating of meat, and indeed for the farming of animals in order to do so.

But if the eating of meat in order to sustain life is justified under natural law, what about the conditions in which the farming of animals takes place? Most species do not have any choice about their feeding habits, they simply catch what they can. The human species, on the other hand, controls the production of animals for food. Does such control imply moral responsibility?

An example:

A cat will torment, kill and eat a mouse. The sight of it doing so might be extremely distasteful, but it is the cat's nature to do so. However much the cat may have been domesticated, it is still a natural hunter, and its instincts are to kill.

If I decide to take a pet mouse out of its cage, set it free in a room and then chase after it, biting it from time to time, before killing and eating it, I would be considered to be acting in a way that is unnatural, and the morality of having such a supper would be questioned. My feeding habits might feature in a tabloid newspaper, and I might find myself under pressure to accept psychotherapy. I would certainly be banned from keeping pet mice.

- What distinguishes me from the cat in this respect?

- Does my rationality and ability to choose other sources of food mean that I therefore have a moral responsibility towards the mouse?

- If I were starving, would I then be morally justified in eating the mouse?

The treatment of animals is connected with questions about diet and standards of living. If fresh meat is enjoyed occasionally, and a roast chicken is regarded as a delicacy, it becomes more possible to breed chickens in humane circumstances – since fewer are needed and people will pay more for what is considered a delicacy. On the other hand, if it is expected that people will eat meat every day, and chicken portions are consumed on all occasions, then the demand for quantity of such meat goes up, and artificial methods are therefore found to maximise the efficiency of 'meat production'.

A change in attitude to animals therefore implies a change in eating habits and expectations, even aside from the issue of vegetarianism.

How do you assess the fairness of an implied contract in which a member of one species is born, reared and fattened, and then killed to feed members of another species? All the gains would seem to be on one side. The animal used for food is not considered as an individual member of a species, but simply as a source of protein.

EXPERIMENTS ON ANIMALS

In an opinion poll of teenagers, carried out in Britain in 1993, the action to which the largest number objected (90 per cent) was killing animals for their fur. But second to this was testing cosmetics on animals (89 per cent). This came well ahead of using animals in medical experiments, to which 69 per cent objected.

Using a utilitarian argument, the gains to be anticipated must outweigh the pain inflicted. Thus, if it is possible to use an animal in a test which might result in finding a cure for a serious disease, then many people would judge that a morally acceptable thing to do. Of course, it would need to be shown that no more suffering than was necessary was inflicted on the animals concerned.

On the other hand, the testing of cosmetics on animals does not yield life-saving benefits. Cosmetics are not essential to life – the use of cosmetics which have been tested on animals is therefore optional, a matter of personal moral choice. One teenager, campaigning for the use of cruelty-free cosmetics, used the slogan

'Make up your mind before you make up your face' – highlighting the nature of the choice involved.

Therefore, using a combination of a natural respect for the life of animals, and a utilitarian approach to the expected gains from experimentation, the main moral question about animal experimentation may be set out as:

- Is it necessary to use animals in these tests, or is there some other way to obtain the same information?

- Are the tests carried out in such a way as to minimise the pain caused?

- Are the anticipated results of the tests of sufficient importance to justify the suffering involved?

— THE NATURAL ENVIRONMENT —

In almost all moral thinking, the ultimate criterion has been human happiness – directly so in the case of utilitarianism, indirectly in the natural law arguments, intuitionism or the categorical imperative. It is assumed that moral choices are about the avoidance of pain. We seek to benefit humans first of all, and then, by extension, may feel some responsibility towards other species. On the other hand, a stone cannot feel pain, or express a preference. Therefore, it may be ignored in most moral debate. From a utilitarian point of view, care of the environment has therefore been seen as a moral issue first and foremost because destruction of the environment involved harm to humankind.

An example:

- If rain-forests are destroyed, we may be concerned because

  - global warming will effect us all

  - many medicines are discovered through analysis of rare plant species, many of which are still to be found in the rain-forests

---

A second approach is implied by what has already been said about the 'natural law' argument. Whether backed by religious convictions or not, there may be a sense that everything – humans, other species, the planet itself – has its place within an overall scheme of things which we glimpse, but neither fully understand nor control.

This is essentially metaphysics – it goes beyond descriptions of the physical environment to consider issues of value and meaning. It may see the world as something to be valued, treasured even, quite apart from any specific or demonstrable benefit to humankind.

With such an approach, all sentient beings are given a measure of respect – all are to be treated in a way which strives to allow them to have a life which is appropriate to their species.

> ***Examples:***
>
> • Is it right to keep wild animals caged in zoos?
>
> • Is the concept of making an animal into a 'pet' one that does violence to the animal's original nature?
>
> • Should we breed favourite species on grounds of aesthetic appeal?

A problem with a utilitarian assessment of our moral responsibilities to other species or to the environment as a whole is that the human happiness it seeks may be relatively short lived. We are unable to tell the long-term effects of environmental change on humankind.

We have to recognise, however, that the human species, both by its numbers and its technology, has produced massive changes to the environment. Many of these have been justified in terms of human development and a utilitarian assessment of happiness. An alternative view – in which the human species is one of many, and does not automatically have a right to dominate all others – is an attitude that springs from a fundamental sense of the meaning and purpose of life. But such a view brings us close to the sphere of religion, to which we now turn.

10

—— RELIGION AND —— MORAL VALUES

The moral choices people make, and the values they express through them, depend (consciously or unconsciously) on their understanding of the nature of the world and the place of humankind within it. But these are also things with which religions are concerned.

Each religion:

- presents a particular view of the world;

- promotes a set of values by which its followers should live;

- gives specific advice on how to live – either in terms of rules to be followed, or attitudes to be taken.

Religious rules or values may be based on:

- the authority of a religious leader or holy book;

- the cumulative experience of that religious community;

- rational thought, or an understanding of what is 'natural'.

Ethics is the rational examination of moral choices – so part of what religious morality offers (the part that depends on reason) is ethics. But the values that religion promotes may have an influence far beyond those who are actually practising members of that religion.

So, for example, many of the ethical arguments that we have examined so far are based on ideas and values that have been promoted by the Christian religion. This does not mean that every ethical thinker is Christian, but that everyone who lives within Western culture is liable to be influenced by Christian ideas, simply because they have come to pervade so much of our habitual thinking. The same would be true for someone living in a predominantly Jewish, Muslim, Hindu, Sikh or Buddhist society – the assumptions people make about the nature and value of life often reflect their religious background, or a deliberate reaction against it.

HOW ARE RELIGION AND MORALITY RELATED?

There are three possibilities:

1. **autonomy**   Morality may be autonomous if it is based on reason alone, without any reference to religious ideas. If its values are the same as a particular religion, that is seen as purely coincidental.

2. **heteronomy**   Morality may be said to be heteronomous (i.e. rules coming from outside itself) if it depends directly upon religious belief, or on a set of values given by religion.

3. **theonomy**   Morality is theonomous (i.e. comes from God) if both it and religion are thought to come from a common source of inspiration and knowledge – a source which religion might refer to as 'God'.

SOME ARGUMENTS IN FAVOUR OF AUTONOMY:

- Responsible moral choice depends on freedom and the ability to choose rationally. But some religions have inculcated rules that should be obeyed out of fear of punishment. Rewards and punishments may be offered after this life – either in terms of heaven or hell, or in terms of rebirth into higher or lower forms of life. With such religious pressure, can a person be truly free or moral?

- Different religions (or even different sects within a single religion) often take different approaches to moral issues. There is no clear guidance. In order to choose between conflicting religious views, a person has to use his or her reason as the ultimate deciding factor – which is autonomy!

- If I subscribe to one of the theistic religions (i.e. I believe in God), then I will believe that God already knows what I will choose to do before I myself choose to do it. If he is all-powerful, he should be able to prevent me from doing what is wrong. If he does not do so, he is responsible for the consequences of my action, aiding and abetting me through divine negligence! In which case, I lose my moral responsibility.

SOME ARGUMENTS IN FAVOUR OF HETERONOMY:

- People cannot escape from the influence of religious values and attitudes. They have an unconscious effect, even for those who reject religion. Better, then, to acknowledge that influence than try to deny it.

- As soon as you try to define moral terms (such as 'goodness' or 'justice') you are using language which has been shaped by the prevailing religions. Natural law, for example, may have come originally from Aristotle, but today it is understood largely through the use made of it by Aquinas and the Catholic Church. Religion has largely supplied the language of ethical debate.

- It is one thing to understand what is right, quite another to have the courage or conviction to put it into effect. It can be argued that religion is the source of such courage and conviction, and that it provides a society within which values and moral attitudes can be shared and reinforced.

- Philosophers often assume that everyone is reasonable. Religions, by contrast, are well aware of human selfishness and unreasonableness. Religion is likely to offer a more realistic view of human nature than philosophy, and will therefore be better able to guide moral choice.

SOME ARGUMENTS IN FAVOUR OF THEONOMY:

- Intuitionism was right in saying that there are certain things that are known, but cannot be described. We have an intuitive sense of the meaning of the word 'good' – and this intuition lies behind both the ideas and practice of religion, and also the impulse to understand ethics.

- It can be argued that religion and morality have a common source in 'mystical' experience – moments of intuitive awareness of a sense of meaning, purpose of wholeness in life, of well-being and acceptance. This is a basic feature of religious experience, and also gives the impetus to act in a purposeful and moral way.

- Metaphysics (the rational exploration of meaning and purpose in the world) can be seen as a basis for morality (as in Greek thought, in the 'natural law' tradition, and as explored today by, for example, Iris Murdoch in *Metaphysics as a Guide to Morals*) and also as fundamental to religion.

- Ideas like 'categorical imperative' and 'conscience', imply the personal awareness of obligation and meaning that are also fundamental to religion.

The essential difference between secular ethics and religious morality, however they may be related, is that secular ethics justifies moral choice through rational argument, whereas religious morality regards moral choice as an expression of its fundamental beliefs and values.

Each of the world religions has a distinctive way of presenting the values by which its followers seek to live, so it is important to explore them individually. In each of the sections that follow, we shall look at the way in which that religion argues for its general moral principles and values.

There is no scope within this book to look in any systematic way at the actual lifestyle, attitudes or values of each religion - these can be found set out in books on the individual religions (e.g. the *Teach Yourself World Faiths* series). Our task here is to examine not so much *what* they value, as *why* they value it, and how they therefore justify their moral attitudes.

JUDAISM

Jewish morality is based on the *Torah*, which means 'Teaching' or 'Law'. It is found in the first five books of the Hebrew Bible, and includes many rules for ethical and social matters. The most famous of these rules are the Ten Commandments (Exodus 20:1-17), and the Torah was famously summed up by Rabbi Hillel in the first century BCE in one of the various forms of the 'golden rule' – 'What is hateful to you do not do to another'.

The body of Torah developed over the centuries, as each law was applied to new situations. Eventually (by about 600CE) a complex encyclopedia of rules and traditions, the *Talmud,* was completed. It contains the *Mishna*, a collection of oral traditions, believed to have been originally given to Moses by God, along with the written Torah, plus further commentaries on the Mishna, called the *Gemara*.

Jews are required to follow these in the correct way, and this is called the *halakah*, or 'path'. Different groups within Judaism vary in the strictness with which they put these rules into effect. Some take them literally in every detail, others follow rather more general principles, adapting where necessary to some perceived requirements of modern life.

In terms of morality, the Jewish approach is one of rules. Reason and conscience have their part to play, but mainly in terms of interpretation and application.

It is important to emphasise, however, that the rules are not regarded as arbitrary. They are seen as having the authority of God, given to humankind for its benefit. The many layers of tradition which surround the original Torah represent the cumulative experience of generations. There is a real sense that, in keeping the rules of his or her religion, a follower of the Jewish faith is not simply adopting a particular style of life, but entering into a community and a tradition.

─────── CHRISTIANITY ───────

Since it developed out of Judaism (Jesus having been a Jew, and his first followers having formed a sect within Judaism, rather than a separate religion), Christianity accepts the moral basis of the Ten Commandments, and the Jewish Torah is part of its own scriptures.

Christianity interprets the rules of the Torah in the light of the life and teaching of Jesus Christ. In the New Testament, a significant feature of this is that Jesus was prepared to set aside the detailed requirements of the Law, but insisted that, in doing so, he was not setting the Law aside, but rather fulfilling and completing it. This has allowed Christian morality a measure of interpretive flexibility.

Early in the history of the Christian Church it was agreed that its members should not be required to keep all the rules of the Torah (the crucial issue being the distinctively Jewish practice of circumcision), thus allowing Gentiles to accept an equal place with Jews in the new religion. Nevertheless, Christians and Jews hold a core of moral tradition in common.

Christianity emphasises faith in God and in Jesus Christ, rather than obedience to religious rules, as the basis of its way of life. It is therefore less rule-based than Judaism, even where it shares the same values.

Sources of authority for Christian morality vary from one Christian denomination to another. But they include:

- The authority of the Church (believed to be inspired by the Holy Spirit), including the Pope, the Bishop of Rome.

- The authority of the Scriptures.

- Human reason (used in applying a 'natural law' basis for morality).

- Conscience.

- The direct inspiration of the Holy Spirit.

The fact that there are a number of different sources of authority is significant. Thus, at the time of the Reformation, the authority of the Church was challenged on the basis of the authority of the Scriptures. Reason and conscience are significant in re-examining the relevance of particular teachings to changing cultural and social circumstances.

ISLAM

The word 'Islam' means 'submission'. Muslims believe that most things in the word submit naturally to God, the source of life. Humankind is the exception, for people can either choose to submit to God, living in a natural way, or can refuse to do so. Fundamental to Muslim ethics is the idea that everything shouid submit in a natural way to the life of the universe. Indeed, Muslims believe that every child is born a Muslim, and only later may adopt another religion, or decide to have no religion at all.

Muslims believe that Allah (the Arabic term for God, the source of life) revealed his will for humankind through various prophets (including Jesus, and figures from the Jewish scriptures), but that his final revelation was given through the Prophet Muhammad.

Muslims have two written sources of authority:

1. **The Qur'an** – This is believed by Muslims to be the revelation the will of God, given to Muhammad in a series of visionary experiences. It is traditionally thought that Muhammad was illiterate, but that he was told to recite what he heard. The Qur'an is the written record of that recitation.

2. **The Hadith** – This is a collection of the sayings and deeds of the Prophet Muhammad.

These form the basis of *Shariah*. This term, which means 'path', describes a natural law, created by God, which determines everything in the universe, from the movement of planets to the details of how people should act. Shariah is both an ethical system, a legal framework, and a whole way of life. As far as human beings are concerned, the Shariah is based on three things:

- the Qur'an
- the Sunnah (traditions) of the Prophet
- the natural unity of God.

As they apply the Shariah to present day situations, Muslims apply the principle of analogy – linking a present issue to a decision found in the Hadith or Qur'an. Where there is doubt about what is right, a gathering of Muslim scholars (called the *ulama*) are called together to reach a decision on a point of law. Muslims believe that their community can never agree together upon something that is wrong; therefore, decisions by the *ulama* are authoritative.

One particular feature of Muslim moral thinking is the defence of the faith of Islam and of the community of Muslims. This is called *jihad* (which is often translated as 'holy war', but which means something more like 'striving'). The most common use of *jihad* is an internal one: Muslims are required to strive to overcome their own faults. But they are also required to defend the community and the faith by all means necessary, and this may include going to war. It is also the reason why a death sentence may be passed on someone who is thought to be directly attacking the faith of Islam (as happened in the case of Salman Rushdie, author of *The Satanic Verses*).

Notice how this view contrasts with the libertarian approach of J S Mill, as outlined above in the chapter on 'Law and Order'. For Mill, everyone should be free to express his or her own opinions, even if they are obviously misguided. For him, freedom of the individual takes precedence over the dissemination of right views. For a Muslim this can never be the case – defending the truth of Islam takes absolute priority.

HINDUISM

Hinduism is the name used for a variety of religious traditions that originated in the Indian sub-continent. People do not generally call themselves 'Hindu', but say that they are devotees of Krishna, Shiva or one of the other gods.

Because of this, it is difficult to set out ethical guidelines that will apply in detail to all who might be called Hindu. There are scriptures that are used by a large number of them (the Ramayana or the Bhagavad Gita, for example) but there is no set way of interpreting them, and some Hindus do not read scriptures, but depend on oral traditions for understanding their religion.

Nevertheless, there are certain features that apply widely, and concepts that may be used in understanding the personal and social values of Hindu society.

DHARMA

This is the term used for 'right conduct' or 'duty', and it is this that determines what is morally right. Your particular Dharma depends on who you are, and what stage of life you have reached.

CASTE

Hindu society is divided up into caste groups, within each of which there are various sub-groups. The main groups are:

Brahmin – the priestly caste, generally the most highly educated, and traditionally much involved with education and religion.

Kshatriya – traditionally the warrior caste, these tend to be involved in military and administrative posts, and in the Law.

Vaishya – the 'merchant' caste, often involved with business and agriculture.

(Today there is flexibility between the castes. Some Kshatriyas, for example, hold university teaching posts. What is important to recognise is that those who are born into one of these three castes may be expected to have a sense of their social duty and social position.)

Shudra – this is the caste for manual workers.

Below the four castes come those who are outside the caste system, who tend to take the most menial of work.

THE ASHRAMAS

The Ashramas are the four stages in life. Each of them has certain duties, and each implies certain moral choices:

1. **Student** At this stage a person is expected to work hard, to show respect to parents and teachers, and to develop self-discipline. Students are expected to abstain from sex, alcohol, tobacco and drugs.
2. **Householder** During the middle years of life a person is expected to be involved with marriage, family and career. The social rules for this stage are the most lenient.
3. **Retired** Traditionally, from the time of the arrival of a grandchild, it is expected that both husband and wife may start to stand back from family and business concerns. At this point they may well choose to hand over control of a family business, for example, to the next generation.
4. **Ascetic** A very few Hindus, in the last years of their life, choose to divest themselves of all possessions, and devote themselves to the practise of their religion. Most remain in the retired stage, however, and live with their families.

Hinduism recognises that different people have different abilities, and are able to take on different responsibilities. It does not pretend that society is uniform, or that an equal distribution of goods, or equal rights, will in itself produce happiness or justice.

There are situations in which the caste system allows some people to remain in poverty, or favours those of higher birth even if they do not necessarily have the ability to match their position. But the caste system is not meant to promote inequality, but difference. People are to be given respect, whatever their place in society. Nevertheless, although Hindus may be hard-working and ambitious, their aspirations may well be determined as much by birth as by the actual opportunities afforded by society.

BUDDHISM

Unlike most other religious traditions, Buddhism is not based on a belief in God, but offers a practical set of guidelines for spiritual development.

A Buddhist may say that his or her aim in life is to overcome the suffering caused by greed, hatred and illusion, whilst developing in a way that leads to peace, joy and insight. Buddhists believe that all ethically significant actions (*karma*) have their consequences. What you do today will effect the sort of person you become tomorrow – not in the sense that there is any externally imposed law to that effect, but just because actions have their natural consequences. Those who are foolish remained trapped in a cycle of craving and unsatisfactoriness.

Buddhists try to cultivate qualities of compassion, gentleness and serenity. They are seen as the ideals by which individual Buddhists are inspired to shape their lives.

Buddhist moral guidelines are summed up in the five basic precepts which all committed Buddhists undertake to follow:

- not to destroy life

  This will mean avoiding the killing of other humans, and also (for many Buddhists) keeping to a vegetarian diet, so as to minimise the suffering of other species. It also implies that Buddhists should avoid a negative attitude towards life – denigrating people or situations – but should cultivate an attitude of *metta* (loving kindness)

- not taking what is not given

  This requires the avoidance of dishonesty, but also the grasping for material goods in a way that may be honest, but implies craving. In place of it, Buddhists are to cultivate an attitude of generosity.

- not indulging in harmful sexual activity

  Except for those who have chosen to accept the discipline of a monastic way of life, there is only the general principle that sexuality should not be used in such a way as to harm people. Although many Buddhist attitudes are shaped by the cultures within which it has developed, in general, Buddhism takes a liberal and positive attitude to sex – although those who aspire to follow the spiritual path seriously may find that they are able to find personal fulfilment without sexual activity.

* not saying what is not true

Buddhists should avoid lying, or deliberately giving a false impression, but should always try to be aware of and express the truth.

* not to take those things which cloud the mind

In order to increase their awareness, it is important that Buddhists should stay alert and be sensitive to their own and other people's feelings and responses. This cannot happen if the mind is dulled by alcohol or drugs, and so it is recommended to avoid them. There is no absolute prohibition, however, as in Islam.

As well as these principles, Buddhists are required to cultivate four mental states:

Love: towards all creatures and towards oneself

Pity: compassion for all who suffer

Joy: an unselfish sharing in the happiness of others

Serenity: freeing oneself from anxieties of success or failure, and being equal minded in dealing with other people.

Buddhists do not refer to actions as 'good' or 'bad', 'right' or 'wrong', but as 'skilful' or 'unskilful'. This implies that an action is assessed by the intention of the person who does it, rather than by any external absolutes. An action is skilful if it is the result of insight and loving kindness, it is unskilful if it is the result of ignorance, greed or hatred. That unskilfulness is shown both in the action itself, and also in the results that come from it.

—————————— SIKHISM ——————————

Sikhs believe that, without the inspiration that comes from devotion to God, people live in illusion and are dominated by the five evil impulses: lust; anger; greed; attachment to worldly things; pride. Sikhs are therefore required to cultivate their opposites:

- self-control
- forgiveness
- contentment
- love of God
- humility.

In practical terms, the guidelines for the Sikh way of life are set out in a book called the *Rehat Maryada: A Guide to the Sikh Way of Life*, a translation of a Punjabi work of 1945, produced by a group of Sikh scholars and regarded as authoritative for giving a summary of the Sikh way of life, and the teachings of the ten Gurus upon which the Sikh faith is based.

The Sikh community is concerned to emphasise equality. Every Gurdwara (a place of Sikh worship) has a kitchen and a place where worshippers can sit and eat together. This is a way of demonstrating the unity and equality of Sikhs.

Sikhs who belong to the Khalsa (those who have committed themselves in a ceremony to follow the Sikh way of life – the word itself means 'pure') are required to carry a sword (kirpan), to be used in self-defence. It should be used only when all peaceful means of resolving a dispute have failed, and only to re-establish justice where there has been a wrong (for example, to defend the Sikh community), or in a direct act of self-defence.

– RELIGIOUS VALUES AND SOCIETY –

In this chapter we have attempted to give no more than the briefest outline of the way in which those who belong to the various faith communities establish the values upon which their moral views depend.

Notice the variety of approaches – not so much in the principles of moral action, for there are some features which all have in common, but in the way in which they are established. Some are imposed by authoritative teachers, or through the interpretation of scriptures. Others depend more on the traditions of their own communities. Some have many specific rules (notably Judaism and Islam), others (notably Buddhism) avoid the concept of rules altogether. Some offer rewards after death for obeying the rules, punishments for those who disobey. Others see actions as bringing about their own consequences without external agency.

Such values and moral principles make most direct sense within the faith communities themselves. There, the shared values and shared moral rules give cohesion to the community.

Where members of a faith community live within a secular society, the moral principles by which that society claims to live may well be similar to those of the faith community, but the actual force of authority and the way in which those rules are justified may be quite different.

An example:

The deliberate killing of another human being is against the law in almost all societies, except in particular circumstances (e.g. when war is declared, or where a person is legally sentenced to death). Now a Buddhist living in that society would also wish to refrain from killing – not because of the secular law, but from a profound respect for all living things. Because the reason for not killing is different, the Buddhist may also oppose those forms of killing which are permitted by society, which includes the killing of animals for food. The superficial observation of people behaving in the same way does not therefore mean that they are following the same moral principles in the same way.

Sometimes moral dilemmas reflect differences of culture, rather than religious belief as such. Traditionally, Asian families have maintained close control over their young people, especially girls. The dilemma is that young Asians in the West may wish to go along with the prevailing culture, to the distress of their families.

An situation:

A 23-year-old Hindu girl is disowned by her family because she has been working as a model, appearing in soft porn magazines. Although she was originally shocked and felt very uncomfortable about appearing topless, she came to accept it and found that it ceased to bother her. She claimed that it did not change her traditional, conservative attitude to sexual morality.

• Is it possible to live equally in two cultures, if they hold conflicting values? Can one be a devout Hindu and yet accept the values of a largely secular Western society?

• Which should take precedence, the individual or the family and cultural group?

This illustrates the problems of ethics in a multi-cultural society – it is not simply a matter of understanding the religious and cultural norms of each group, but of sorting out to which group a person is giving his or her loyalty at any one time.

THE LIMITS OF RELIGIOUS FREEDOM?

There are situations where religious beliefs lead to actions that go against the prevailing norms of the society within which they operate.

Two examples:

1. *In Waco, Texas in 1993, a branch of the Seventh Day Adventist Church, led by David Koresh, was besieged in its headquarters by federal agents, following a shooting incident. The cult members were heavily armed, and there had been a considerable exchange of fire in which four agents has been killed. At the end of the siege there was a fire in which Koresh and many of his followers died.*

2. *Some people refuse to accept medical attention on religious grounds. For example, Jehovah's Witnesses may refuse to accept blood transfusions. They may also refuse treatment to their children on religious grounds. In 1990, a devout Christian Science couple were put on trial in Massachusetts, charged with manslaughter, on the grounds that they did not summon medical help for their two yeur old son, who died of a bowel obstruction in 1986. During his illness he was prayed for by a Christian Science practitioner and looked after by a Church nurse.*

- Should a religious cult be allowed to operate outside the laws of the society within which its members live? Does society as a whole have a right to legislate about religious beliefs?

- Historically, those who have deviated from the norms of religious belief have often been persecuted and killed. In contrast, there is wide acceptance today of the idea that the free practice of one's religion is a basic human right. To what extent is there a moral obligation on society, or on individuals, to monitor or take action to prevent the spread of beliefs which (on the basis of the ethics of society as a whole) are harmful?

SOME CONCLUSIONS

This book has attempted to present a general introduction to some of the major ethical arguments, showing some of the strengths and weaknesses of each in turn. Now, by way of conclusion, I want to draw together some of these main themes and to give my own comments and evaluation.

The opening chapter was called 'The Art of Living'. This was intended to emphasise that the process of making moral choices, and the task of reflecting on the possible justification for them, is a creative and personal activity. Sometimes, when immersed in the details of a utilitarian argument, trying to assess consequences in a detached way, one can lose sight of this feature of moral choice. No matter how clearly the predicted results of an action are presented, people in fact make their own decisions, often in what appears to be an irrational manner. They are responding to things that they value, memories of past actions, past hurts perhaps. They feel compelled by impulses, both conscious or unconscious, to do what they feel they must do. They are sometimes prepared to accept painful consequences, even admit that they are foolish – and yet the choice is made. The actual process of moral choice is by no means simple, and ethics (if it is to be not only a comment on how moral choices are actually made, but also a guide to how moral choices should be made, which is the implication of most ethical arguments) needs to reflect this.

Ethics – moral philosophy – is a rational activity. It studies moral choices, explores their implications and looks at how they may be justified. And therein lies its inherent weakness. It tends to assume, just because it is a rational discipline, that a single theory may be found that will explain the nature of moral thinking and give an overall view of life by which the results of moral thinking may be assessed. Its ideal is to find a definition of good and bad that will transcend individual preferences, and which may therefore command universal acceptance. That is fine in theory, and yet it does not really do justice to the human complexity of moral choice.

The problem has, for some time, been made more complicated by the narrow definition of meaning which dominated philosophy in the earlier part of the 20th century. If a meaning of a statement is given only with reference to things that can be seen and touched – objects 'out there' to be encountered through the senses – or to the definitions of words, then there is little scope for the sort of creativity that is found in moral language. We saw, in Chapter 3, how ethical thinkers have met this challenge and have come to recognise the variety of uses to which moral language is put – giving commands, registering preferences, expressing emotions. Ethics is too fluid and complex an activity to be confined to a language appropriate to science rather than art.

In the chapter on 'natural law' we saw how rational consideration of the final end and purpose of an object or an activity could be used as a touchstone for whether it was being used or abused. It is designed and intended for one right purpose, and anything else is deemed to be wrong. Natural law is clear cut, straightforward. It is a 'clean' theory, attempting to cut through the messiness of human experience. But it is also abstract, cerebral, linked to a philosophy which no longer commands universal acceptance.

Perhaps this was illustrated by the comments in that chapter which indicated that 'natural law' and behaving in a natural way were not always the same thing. There are plenty of things that my nature might incline me to do which would not be approved of by the proponents of the 'natural law' argument! Does that mean that I disagree with the 'end' to which a natural law theory says my life is given? Not necessarily. But it does mean that, at the moment of making a moral choice, I cannot see myself as being only for that 'end'. My nature is ever changing, never that simply defined. It defies being told exactly what its purpose shall be in the whole scheme of things.

When we moved on to utilitarianism, the argument was very different, but the impulse to systematise and quantify remained. The same drive that sought a rational explanation of final cause within the world, now struggled with a definitive balance of happiness offered to the maximum number of people. But again, this rational approach became more complicated because it needed to ask about what constituted happiness, and whether the gains should be immediate or long term, whether confined to the act, or the general rule, or the preferences of those involved. It became a quest for results – a quest which, as one event led on to another, could never be completed.

Common sense tends to go along with utilitarianism. Avoiding suffering and giving happiness are, after all, on an emotional as well as a rational level, deeply embedded in human experience. And yet utilitarianism, in itself, does not seem to be enough. There are so many situations in the world – from the horrors of civil war, to the tragedy of drug abuse – for which, from a logical and utilitarian point of view, there can be no possible justification. Why do those involved not see it? Why do they not stop their spiral of violence and death? Why cannot they accept a utilitarian judgement on their actions, when all the evidence about the consequences of what they do is plain for all to see?

The answer to these questions is that choices are not always rational, and sometimes they are made in the face of known consequences. The expected results of an action inform, but cannot define, a moral choice – they form part of a moral quandary, factors to be weighed, and yet the weighing is not the whole of the experience of choice. To describe someone as 'cold and calculating' or 'hard headed' implies a narrow view of human choices and moral responsibility (such a person could probably give a very definite utilitarian justification of his or her action) and yet the feeling can remain that there is more to the art of living than simply assessing results and acting accordingly.

But what is this elusive 'more' that transforms an action based on calculated results into an act of creative living, of self-affirmation, of agonizing importance for the individual concerned?

Kant approached this 'more' in seeing it as a categorical imperative – as something absolute, not depending on results. He places God, freedom and immortality as presuppositions of moral choice – as background assumptions and ideas that influence moral choice. As we choose what to do, we bring to that process of choice all the ideas and experiences of our past, all our hopes for the future. We may appear to be conditioned, but we experience ourselves as free. We may not know what the results of our action will be, and yet we feel impelled to do it anyway.

Yet Kant offers the most generalised and theoretical of all frameworks for moral choice, that I should will that the maxim of my action become a universal law. Wanting everyone to be able to make the same choice has a common sense basis. If I want to do something, I should allow everyone else to do it as well. That may be part of my deliberations as I decide how to act, but is it everything? I may just be dissuaded by the thought that if everyone else does it there will be chaos. But the truth is that we are all different. It is not realistic to expect or want everyone to make that same moral choice. I know that my choice is not, in actual fact, going to be enacted as a universal law – and this remains in the back of my mind, even if I try to consider the implications of making it so. At the end of the day, I go ahead and make my choice as a unique individual. Universalising every moral decision, and acting only on those that can be universalised, is likely, it would seem to me, to produce a lowest common denominator of moral thinking: the blandest of moral visions. It is hardly the stuff of which 'the art of living' is made.

We looked at morality from the standpoint of personal development. And here there came a perspective that was closest to the idea of 'the art of living', for here was moral choice being used and justified in terms of its function of creating and expressing the human will. But that perspective alone was not enough – a world full of egocentric individuals, each determined to pursue his or her own development, is not a welcome prospect. We therefore explored the social and legal perspective on morality, and then on the global issues and the special problems they raised.

Finally, we looked at the ways in which the world religions formulated their values and moral principles. Without being able to explore exactly what each religion would say about each moral issue, it was at least clear that some worked on the basis of detailed legislation, others on general rules, on flexible social requirements, or on whether an action was skilful in leading to spiritual development. The religions provide a wide measure of consensus on the general values that enhance human life, and each of them provide their own form of 'the art of living'.

So where does this leave us?

The moral choices people make are based on many things, but they are rooted in an understanding of the nature of the world, and the values that arise from that understanding. For some people this is well thought out and rational; for others it is provided by a religion and accepted ready made; others act instinctively, their understanding and valuation of the world working through the unconscious.

In the broadest sense, this is metaphysics: the quest to understand the meaning of the world as a whole. This is the process that lay behind the 'natural law' arguments, but it can be broader than the world view of Aristotle on which that theory was based.

The moment of moral choice is therefore informed by the way in which we generally understand and value life. In her book *The Sovereignty of Good* 1970, Iris Murdoch expressed it in this way:

'We act rightly "When the time comes" not out of strength of will but out of a quality of our usual attachments and with the kind of energy and discernment which we have available. And to this the whole activity of our consciousness is relevant.' [p53]

To ask 'What should I do?' implies the question 'What is life for?'. Life is constantly changing; nothing at all, not even our galaxy, remains fixed for ever. We can try to run from this truth – craving absolutes that will justify our decisions for all time – but it is an illusion. Constant change is a reality, and it affects not just the world around us, but we ourselves. We are not fixed as individuals, our minds shape the future – the choices we make today define the sort of people we become tomorrow. We also have to accept that life, however much we shape it to suit our own ends, involves suffering and death. We can work to minimise suffering and promote happiness; but we cannot remove the fact that humans are limited and fragile creatures. Fallibility and failure are not just an accidental feature of life that should be quickly removed and forgotten – they are a feature of living in this sort of world, in which human aspirations outstrip human abilities.

Does this imply moral scepticism? Does it mean that there are no absolutes in terms of right or wrong? Is every individual responsible for constructing his or her own values and morality? Does everyone start from scratch and re-invent the moral wheel?

I do not think this follows from what I have said about the uniqueness of the situation of moral choice. Every choice, whether its roots are recognised consciously or not, is informed by many things – values and an understanding of life that we have gathered through education, through the influence of others, and through personal experience. The individual decision may therefore be unique, but that which informs it is part of our common inheritance of wisdom or folly.

In conclusion, I would sum up the quest for 'the art of living' in this way:

- Moral choices are based on the beliefs, the values and the general understanding of life of the people who make them.

- Every choice is unique. General rules never fully encompass the actual situations in which people find themselves.

- Ethics – the rational examination of moral choice – needs to recognise the complexity of such choices. No single theory, no single approach, no single perspective will do justice to that process.

- Our mind can respond to the world in one of two ways. It can be creative or reactive. A reactive mind responds to external stimuli. A creative mind looks at the stimuli, evaluates them and uses its power and freedom to shape life, within the limitations of human life and change.

- A moral choice is therefore a creative act. It changes the world – even if by only an infinitesimal amount. Every act of heroism or of brutality affects the lives of those it touches: after it, the world is never quite the same.

The relationship between ethics and the moral life is rather like that between literary theory and the creative writer, or between musical theory and the act of composition. Writer and composer use all their feelings, intuitions, values and insights to produce a work of art that is unique. Later, the theorists analyse it, place it in within categories, show influences.

Ethics is rather like that. It analyses moral choices and devises theories to show how they may be justified. It is a valuable process, a useful guide for future action, but it can never fully explain the process of creative living.

– SUGGESTIONS FOR –
FURTHER READING

Many of the important texts in the history of Ethics have been mentioned in this book. It is well worth reading at least extracts from these, in order to get a flavour of how the ideas of various philosophers were originally presented. For example:

Plato, *The Republic*

Aristotle, *The Nicomachean Ethics*

Machiavelli, *The Prince*

Hobbes, *Leviathan*

Hume, *A Treatise on Human Nature*

Bentham, *An Introduction to the Principles of Morals and Legislation*

Kant, *Fundamental Principles in the Metaphysics of Morals* and *The Critique of Practical Reason*

Mill, *Utilitarianism*

Nietzsche, *Thus Spoke Zarathustra* and *Beyond Good and Evil*

Moore, *Principia Ethica*

This is no more than a selection of those mentioned in this book, and does not include the many important modern writers on

Ethics. Many other important thinkers, for example Augustine, Aquinas or Kierkegaard, deserve careful study by those who want to explore the subject further. Useful extracts from a number of these texts can be found in, for example:

Johnson, O A; *Ethics: Selections from Classical and Contemporary Writers* (4th edition) Holt, Reinhart and Winston, 1978.

There are other useful books that give an introduction to ethics from a historical perspective, for example:

Norman, R; *The Moral Philosophers,* OUP, 1983.

[This has sections on 'The Ancients' (Plato; Aristotle), 'The Moderns' (Hume; Kant; Mill; Hegel) and some modern themes, including, usefully, 'Ethics and Marxism' and 'Ethics and Psychoanalysis'.]

MacIntyre, A; *A Short History of Ethics*, Routledge and Kegan Paul, 1967.

Warnock, G J; *Contemporary Moral Philosophy,* Macmillan, 1967.

[This is a particularly useful outline with critical comment on modern ethical theories.]

Other useful books for a general introduction to ethical issues include:

Mayo, Bernard; *The Philosophy of Right and Wrong,* Routledge & Kegan Paul, 1986.

Murdoch, Iris; *Metaphysics as a Guide to Morals,* OUP, 1992.

Nuttall, Jon; *Moral Questions: An Introduction to Ethics,* Polity Press, Cambridge, 1993.

Porter, B E; *Reasons for Living,* Macmillan, 1988.

Singer, P; *Practical Ethics,* CUP 1979.

[This book is now out of print, but it clearly sets out moral argument on a useful variety of topics]

Mackie, J L; *Ethics: Inventing Right and Wrong,* Penguin, 1977.

Thompson, Mel; *ATP10: Ethics,* Hodder & Stoughton, 1991.

  [This is a teaching pack, with worksheets, for those taking A level and similar courses in Ethics.]

For the religious dimension of moral thought, see, for example:

Teach Yourself World Faiths – a series of *Teach Yourself* books, one on each of the major world religions, highlighting the moral and social attitudes of members of the faith communities.

There are a wide range of school textbooks covering moral issues, including:

Chignell, M A; *Perspectives,* Hodder & Stoughton, 1981.

Thompson, Mel; *Guidelines for Life,* Hodder & Stoughton, 1990.

Jenkins, Joe; *Contemporary Moral Issues,* Heinemann, 1992.

INDEX